Godly Glimpses

Discoveries
of the Love That Heals

Peggy Eastman

Our Sunday Visitor Publishing Division
Our Sunday Visitor, Inc.
Huntington, Indiana 46750

Year 2000 Edition, Copyright © 1999 by Peggy Eastman

To order: Call toll-free 1-800-348-2440, Ext. 2460

ISBN: 0-87973-593-7
LCCCN: 99-70513

Cover design by Rebecca Heaston
Cover and section photographs by Rudolf A. Ruda
PRINTED IN THE UNITED STATES OF AMERICA

593

For Jim and Rudy

Contents

Acknowledgments

I would like to thank all the people who helped me bring *Godly Glimpses* from dream to printed reality; I hope you know who you are in your hearts. While it would be impossible to name everyone who helped, I would especially like to thank Charles Roth and Jacquelyn M. Lindsey, acquisitions editor at Our Sunday Visitor, who saw the potential of this book from the beginning, and my editor Henry F. O'Brien, Our Sunday Visitor's managing editor of religious books. I would also like to thank Eunice Riles, Grace Rinaldi, Grace DiCairano, Edna Jane Nolte, Rayola McLaughlin, Mary Murray, and all the Catholic Daughters of the Americas; Annette P. Kane, executive director of the National Council of Catholic Women; my parents, Isabelle and Jack Barr; my brother, John L. Barr, M.D.; my aunt, Ann Barr Perkins; and Henry G. "Hank" Harris, an Episcopalian priest. For specific support on this book I owe a debt to Virginia Pettebone, Linda Foley, Kathryn Abell, Kathleen Williams, and the late John A. Kuett. For personal and spiritual nourishment I am indebted to Jill H. Barr, the All Saints Church Bereavement Group, the Monday Night Scripture Study Group, the Third Tuesday Book Club, the Wednesday night church potluck group, and Ronald and Jo Carlberg.

I would also like to thank the publishing professionals who have helped guide me along the way. While I cannot name them all, I would especially like to thank the following: James McDermott and the editors at *Guideposts* magazine; Ric Cox, executive editor of *Plus* magazine; Father Allan Weinert, editor of *Liguorian* magazine; Dianne Partie Lange, now a contributing editor at *Allure* magazine; Susan Roy, health editor of *SELF* magazine; John A. Limpert, editor of *Washingtonian* magazine; John Pekkanen, now a contributing editor at *Reader's Digest*; Elliot Carlson, editor of the *AARP Bulletin*; Serena Stockwell, editor in chief of targeted periodicals at Lippincott Williams & Wilkins; and Karla Wheeler of KS Communications.

Grateful acknowledgment is made to the following for permission to reprint previously published material, some of which appeared in a different form:

Preface

We are all spiritual wayfarers.

We struggle on, sometimes feeling very alone as our feet stumble and our hearts falter. We try to find our way, looking for glimpses of God that will point us in the right direction. These divine moments nourish and strengthen our souls. They can come from within: an inner nudge, a feeling, a flash of insight as bright as a lighted match. Or they can come from without: another person's outstretched hand, the blooming of snowdrops in February, the face of a child, a Psalm that speaks to the heart, or one of earth's small furry creatures, of which you'll meet two, Honey and Jessie, in this book.

Sometimes godly glimpses are as large and unmistakable as highway signs. Sometimes they are so tiny we would miss them entirely if we did not stop and look — just there, by that tree — listen and feel. Sometimes unexpected or unlikely glimpses of God change our course from what we originally intended. Sometimes there seem to be no glimpses of the divine at all and we believe there is no hope of finding any course for our bereft souls. That is how I felt when my life was shattered into shards by the loss of my first husband in a plane crash in 1985, and the loss of my second husband to cancer in 1994. The plane crash was a brutal, garish public drama, for it was the same crash that claimed the life of a young peacemaker named Samantha Smith. Samantha was the Maine schoolgirl invited to visit then-Communist Russia when she wrote to its leader asking why there couldn't be world peace. The death of my second husband was a long, soul-wrenching good-bye, as I watched cancer devour his strength, his smile, and finally his life.

I am a trained medical writer who spent six months on a science-writing fellowship at the U.S. government's National Institutes of Health, the largest scientific research institution in the world. But I found science no help at all for my soul sickness. There seemed to be no prescription for what I suffered.

Like any human being in spiritual crisis, I wrestled with the "why" questions and with my rage at God and His cold-shoulder universe. I sat up late at night in bed, uncomfortable against two pillows, sleepless, thumbing through a worn black Bible. Sometimes the tears dripped on its thin tissue pages. Sometimes I threw it down on the bed, finding no comfort or guidance.

I was sure that I had been abandoned by an uncaring God. Why else would I be consigned to this place of unrelenting pain? Despite my rage and despair and the darkness that curtained my soul, I began to see tiny glimmers that told me I might not always be lost. Suffering in a state of heightened sensibilities, I could not ignore these messages of hope.

We all yearn to find glimpses of the divine to guide our way; this human desire cuts across barriers of religion, language, culture, place, and money. The desire for godly glimpses even cuts across personal pain. Whatever name we use, whatever God we pray to, we yearn to think of that divine Presence as an approachable, caring Creator, not as an abstraction in a theological text. We long to believe that that Presence will not leave us comfortless in sorrow, will celebrate our times of joy, and will share Himself through the Scriptures and the people who nurture us from afar or in our daily lives. People like the late Mother Teresa of Calcutta. People like our husbands, wives, parents, friends, and children. People like our pastor. People like our next-door neighbor.

When my life was thrown into a chaotic, careening blackness, I thought I would never, ever be able to glimpse a caring God again. I was wrong. The form and pattern of the divine were always there; I just couldn't see them. This book is the result of a reexamination of happenings, people, dreams, moments with nature, readings, and memories in my life in the light of godly glimpses that told me God had been there all along. Often I was able to see these glimmers only in retrospect, when I reconsidered the tapestry of life with honesty and a mind open to the divine in daily life. My hope for this book is that it will help all of us to be more attuned to our godly glimpses so we can live strengthened and enriched lives, for seeing those glimpses helps us grow and draw closer to the divine.

The last section of this book includes favorite scriptural passages that have proved a window to the divine for me; I've provided some commentary on them so you'll know why they speak to my heart. I've also added some questions for spiritual reflection so you can think about the godly glimpses in your own life, and a discussion guide for small groups written at the request of my friends. Finally, I've issued an invitation toward the end of the book for you to share your godly glimpses with me, and told you how to reach me. I'd love to hear from you.

Peggy Eastman

Part 1

Godly Glimpses
That Heal the Heart

'I Will Not Leave You Comfortless'

My eyes focused on the badges the two uniformed Maryland policemen held out in front of them and my ears heard what they were saying as I stood on the front stoop of my house at 8:00 A.M. on August 26, 1985. I saw and heard — but the enormity of the news and the changes it would bring were too much for my mind to process.

I heard phrases — snatches of words as hurtful as thrown rocks — "plane crash," "wooded part of Maine," "hard-to-reach site," "fire damage," "trouble identifying remains . . ."

"Remains?" The word landed on my consciousness with an almost physical thud. Remains of what? Then it registered that the two men with badges were talking about my husband, James Coburn Eastman. My beloved, Jim Eastman, six feet three, forty-six years old, big booming voice that filled a courtroom with its power, always in motion, hazel eyes that glinted when he saw me, shirttail drifting out of his belt, strong farmer's hands inherited from his Pennsylvania forebears. . . . Remains?

My body shuddered and I burst into a brief and violent explosion of tears, as if I could expel the words I was hearing from my consciousness. A massive weight — as from the pressure of hundreds of cinder blocks piled on one another — descended onto my chest and stayed there. I tried to talk, but all I could do was cough, as if my lungs were trying to dislodge the cinder-block weight.

"Were there . . . any survivors?" I managed to say to the uniformed men with the kind eyes and the harsh words.

"No, I'm afraid not; none," one detective answered.

"Do you have a close neighbor?" The other detective said quickly, walking me into the living room.

"No," I almost whispered.

"Relatives?" he persisted, taking my arm gently and propelling me down on the couch.

"My parents are in Massachusetts," I said, choking, "but I have a brother." I sat on the brown-flowered sofa of my living room — *our* living room — not moving, huddled in a ball, my arms wrapped around myself, wearing one of my husband's tee shirts and worn khaki Bermuda shorts, as one of the detectives called my brother, Jack, to tell him his sister's husband had been killed in the crash of a Bar Harbor Airlines commuter plane near Auburn, Maine, about ten o'clock on the night of August 25. August the twenty-fifth was my brother's birthday; now the celebration of his birth would be . . . what? *What will we do now on Jack's birthday?* I thought fleetingly.

After the detectives left and before my brother came, I made three phone calls, now supernaturally calm, as if I were playing a part in a tragedy on the stage.

The voice of my husband's law partner was high-pitched, and it quavered. He didn't know how bad it was, but he had heard there was a problem with the plane. Someone had called.

"I'm afraid it's over," I said. "There's no mistake."

"Is everything all right?" said my mother from her small stone house on the Atlantic coast.

"No," I said, clutching the phone receiver tightly, "I'm afraid it is not. Jim has been killed in a plane crash."

I dialed the number of Jim's parents in Florida. The unseen cinder blocks were now crushing my chest, forcing air out of my lungs. I was coughing every few minutes. I felt I might die, and the feeling was welcome. Anything to end this pain, this grotesque performance. As I dialed, I thought, *Oh, God, why must You make me do this?* This was the second adult child the Eastmans had lost; Jim's sister Anne, a missionary in the Belgian Congo, had died of breast cancer at the age of thirty-seven. But I knew the call to Jim's parents had to come from me. No one else.

Now a knife seemed to cut into my heart; it cut, lodged there, and twisted.

"I have some very, very bad news," I said to my mother-in-law, whom I loved as a second mother. "Jim has been killed in a plane crash."

"Oh," gasped his eighty-six-year-old mother, not understanding. "How bad is it?"

"Jim is dead," I said.

My aunt, Ann, pressed the small green leather-bound New Testament into my hands. I sat on the same sofa, the one I had sat on after the policemen had brought me the news that the life I had chosen and lived and loved was over. This was the sofa our two dogs (*my* two dogs, I thought with a sudden twist of the knife in my heart) had turned into their favorite resting place, and I could see their black and golden hairs on the upholstery. The center of my life had now shifted crazily, as if someone had lifted the house and failed to set it down straight.

"Peggy, I want you to have this," my aunt said. The New Testament had been a gift from her son, David, when he was at Notre Dame, she said. "What I want you to do is what I have done. Read the passages I've marked. Read them over and over and over. Then read them again." She pressed the little green book into my hands. I took it, then leafed through the pages, not seeing the type. As I did, the book fell open to St. John, chapter 14. This was no accident, I saw; the book naturally spread apart at this place, as if my aunt, a Navy wife, had read this chapter many times.

The phone was now ringing incessantly; someone else must be answering it. The dogs were racing around the room barking. Friends were starting to arrive with hams and casseroles, florists' deliverymen were ringing the doorbell, their arms filled with flowers — purple iris, white puffs of chrysanthemum, yellow daisies, pale pink roses — how could they bloom when my husband was dead?

"I will not leave you comfortless: I will come to you," I read, not really seeing the words of John (14:18, *King James Version*). I read them again. "I will not leave you comfortless: I will come to you." I saw the squiggly pencil mark my aunt had put in the margin by the passage on the page.

Not leave me comfortless? I knew I could not be comforted. I knew myself inconsolable. I felt like an amputee — at least half of me must be missing. I expected to see blood running down my body. To have snatched from me the one thing in all the world I counted precious, more precious than my own life. . . . I wanted to curl into myself and shrink into nothing, turn my face from the faces that looked at me pityingly, knowing what I knew. This could not have happened, not now. There were many more cases to try, Jim pacing around a courtroom and gesturing for the jury, his shirttail escaping; more slopes of diamond-winking powder to ski down together, our tracks intertwined; more hikes to take when the new leaves were turning green along the C & O canal towpath; more intimate times of love before our fireplace on drizzly fall evenings when the rain tapped at our windows seeking to draw out some of our warmth.

Comfortless? I could never be comforted. It had happened. The final parting no happily married person ever thinks of. Just like that. No good-byes, no time to say to him, "Wait a minute, please . . . just one more kiss. . . . Don't go. . . ." I would never see his grin again, never fold his freshly dried undershirts with the scent of the sun on them, never fix him spaghetti, putting in lots of chopped onions because he liked them, never crawl around the bedroom looking under the bed for his misplaced glasses, never scrub his back, buy him a tie, sew a loose button on his camel overcoat, lift a wine glass to his and toast another wedding anniversary. This was the final closing door, the absolute end to all our dreams and plans and hopes for our future. There was to be no hope for me. At the age of forty-three my life was over. I was an instant widow. Phrases skittered through my head. Black widow spider. Widow's weeds. I was a widow. I hated the word.

Into the midst of this chaos, the swirling antic circus that attends the sudden death of a strong, much-loved activist in his prime, walked a tall man dressed in black with a white clerical collar. He was holding a Bible almost as tightly as I clutched the small green New Testament.

"I'm Hank Harris," said the man in black pastoral garb. I had never seen him before.

Desperately, I tried to be polite. "Do you want some . . . coffee?" I asked him, coughing to get that weight off my chest. Coffee — was there any in this suddenly unfriendly house?

He shook his head no, looking at me with dark eyes that mirrored his compassion. Then I remembered. He must be the new assistant at our church. Jim and I had not yet met him. A friend and choir member who had come to know him said we would like him. He was from . . . Toledo, yes, Toledo, Ohio. Who had sent him?

"May I please see a picture of Jim?" he asked quietly.

Picture. My distracted mind tried to cope with this gentle request. Picture. . . ? Of course, in our bedroom. I took the man in black up the stairs.

Someone had put two pale pink roses in a small vase on our night table by our king-size bed, the one we had shared

17

for twenty-one years, the one with two depressions side by side, Jim's deeper because he weighed more than I. An eva-nescent scent of rose petals floated on the air. I lifted my fa-vorite picture of Jim off the dresser and Hank Harris took it gently in both his hands, looking at the smiling eyes that trapped winking lights, the broad grin, the one long, etched crinkle at the corner of my husband's mouth. Jim's energy and vitality spoke out of the picture frame to us as clearly as a voice.

"Yes," said the assistant pastor. "I see now, I understand." And then I took him downstairs.

Hank Harris's hand, the one holding the Bible, trembled slightly as we sat on the sofa in my living room. *He must be nervous,* I thought, and then fleetingly realized that for the first time since the two policemen had come to my front door and loaded their hard, heavy words on my consciousness, I was not huddled into a ball. He must not have done this very much, come into a house where shattered people tried to talk and move and think despite the sudden amputation of parts of their hearts. He must not know what to say, what prayer might reach me, could ever reach me. Maybe I could help him. What to say?

"Do you think you could tell me a little about why you decided to become a pastor?" I heard myself say. Suddenly it seemed very important to know. I could no longer hear the din around me. I knew the phone was ringing and the door-bell was sounding and the door was opening and the dogs were barking, but I heard none of it. I could not take my eyes off his. I sensed in him a self-contained strength despite his nervousness. I had never met him, and yet I felt I knew him.

And then Hank Harris was talking, at first hesitantly, then surely, and chronological time did not seem to exist and he was telling me about how God had called him to do His work, drawn him into an arena where troubled souls needed help. I had the clear, startling sensation that as he talked Hank Harris was being used as a vessel, that God was pour-ing His love on me through this man, a man who could reach me in the rawness of my pain, and that I — in taking what was offered and responding — was helping.

Much later, after Jim's memorial service, Hank Harris told me that my father had called our local church from Massachusetts. My long-time pastor was out of town. My father had told the church secretary that I had mentioned there was a new assistant pastor someone had said I would like. I hardly remembered saying it. That was all. And so the tenuous message had come to Hank Harris in a roundabout way, with no name attached because I did not know his name. He might have been out. The message might have been routed to someone else. Who guided it?

Jesus said, "I will not leave you comfortless." He kept His promise.

A Letter to Jim

For three months after the death of my husband Jim, my body rebelled at the brutality of this loss. I was physically sick; I couldn't sleep, couldn't eat, couldn't get rid of the cinder blocks on my chest, although I coughed continually to dislodge the weight. I cried often; I thought of Jim constantly. I dreamed of him. In the dreams, I clung to him. "Come back," I called.

I curled up into a tight ball of emotional pain. My family and friends tried to help, but I felt unable to respond. I was frozen inside. I devoured letters of sympathy and tributes to my husband, reading them over and over. They provided comfort, but they were only pieces of paper.

Feeling like the emotional amputee I was, I dragged myself to church. This was the church where I had sung in the choir as a girl, where I had been confirmed and married, where Jim's memorial service had been held. The gray stone of the church walls was comforting, solid; I ran my hands over it. I lifted my eyes to the stained-glass windows. Light coming through the window over the altar illuminated the lamb depicted there, giving it the glow and purity of alabaster.

The church became my home, my spiritual refuge. Some days, I crept into the chapel and sat there, all alone, my head bowed, tears running down my face. In that stone building, people began to reach out to me. They invited me to join a new bereavement support group that was being formed for church members who had lost loved ones.

In my pain and isolation, I hesitated, drew back. How could I tell strangers what I was feeling? How could I cry in front of people I didn't know? How could I share the anguish in my heart?

Fearful and sorrowing, I went, as much to please my pastor as to help myself. But there I found others who were in grief, others who seemed to know what the agony of loss felt like. The group became my new family; they understood. I also found a compassionate group leader, church member, and social worker, Judith Ford Bankson, who gave eight weeks of her time to get us started in weekly meetings. Judy was gentle, nonjudgmental; she shared her own feelings of grief for her dead father.

Soon after we started meeting, Judy made a simple suggestion. She asked each of us to write a letter to our dead loved one. She explained that sometimes, when people who love each other have no chance to say good-bye, writing a letter helps to straighten out turbulent feelings that swirl without form. Putting something on paper can help us see more clearly what our loved ones meant to us, she said; a letter becomes a kind of memorial.

One father wrote to his deceased son: "Writing this is one of the most satisfying things I have done since you went to be with the Lord. As I have written, I have felt unusually close to you. Reviewing our life together has been the next best thing to a visit." I was aware that therapists have long known the value of keeping a personal journal, as a way of helping people cope with emotional pain. Writing a letter to a dead loved one is a variation on keeping a private journal relating thoughts and feelings about a devastating loss. In her book *Widow* (out of print), author Lynn Caine describes how she confided her despair to her "paper psychiatrist" (a yellow legal pad on her nightstand) every night. "I know from the huge volume of mail I've received that writing can be therapeutic for every widow," she writes.

Still, I was skeptical. How should I begin my letter? Wouldn't it just make me feel worse? *What's the point*, I thought, *since Jim can't read it?*

But I sat down at my desk on the afternoon of November 25, 1985, three months after Jim's death. The pale winter light came anemically through the windows of my den, lighting the room only partially. The desk and chairs looked dark and forbidding. It was quiet; there was the stillness of waiting. *Oh, Jim*. I thought, *you would have filled this room with the light of your smile. When you were alive, your smile was all I needed, as if it were the source of my energy.*

I rested my head on the desk, my eyes filling with tears. Then, not knowing what I was going to say, I took out some paper and began to write. It was a long time before I stopped. Here is what I wrote to my dead husband:

Dearest Jim,
You left me so suddenly that I never had a chance to ask you how — if something should happen — I would be able to go

on without you. I never had a chance to hear what I think you would have said, in your deep voice: "You can do it."

"Can do" is the phrase that best sums up the legacy you left me. Without that legacy, how could I possibly draw breath now? How could I close my eyes in sleep, rise in the morning? How could I force food into my mouth, swallow it, digest it? How, without your legacy, could I jog on the park paths we took together, serve a tennis ball without you as my doubles partner, smile for others? How could I answer questions about insurance policies and house renovation?

You prepared me for the worst I could imagine: life without you. You, who taught me to pitch my tent on a precipitous granite bluff in Wyoming's Wind River Mountains among sun-whitened elk bones. You, who taught me the value of tough love: love that demands the best a person has to offer others. You never let me give less than that, no matter what I did.

Do not worry about me, as I do not worry about you. I know where you are, and someday we will be reunited. At that time, I want you to be proud of me and my accomplishments here, even as I want my Savior to know I did not collapse in a heap of energy-sapping self-pity under the worst possible blow that could fall on me. I want you to be able to say, "Well done, Peggy."

It would comfort me to know that you are looking down on me with love and concern, as you looked at me in life. That would make me feel less bereft and less alone. It would also comfort me to think that sometimes I'm hearing your voice, your always-sensible advice guiding me to do something reasonable.

Since your death, only God has taken your place in my heart, and I have welcomed Him in. He loves me, carries my burdens, fills the void left by your passing with His compassionate care. I have read, over and over, the healing words of John 14:18: "I will not leave you comfortless: I will come to you."

You made a strong, positive statement with your life, my dearest Jim. You lived life fully: at a hundred twenty miles an hour. You served as a mentor to me and to many others — that was your spiritual gift. It is apparent in the stacks of letters I've received since you died. You had no class consciousness. Law clerks, secretaries, and court reporters benefited from your caring hand, as did junior and senior partners.

Now I'm asked to go on without my mentor, best friend,

lover, and confidant. I hate it. Being a widow is the absolute pits. Widows and orphans are the lowest of the low. That's why Jesus mentions us by name so many times in the Bible.

I tried always to be there when you needed me. But at the last minute of your earthly life and the last breath of your passing, I was not by your side. Someone else was sitting on the plane next to you. This worries and deeply saddens me. If we had been together, maybe I could have eased the transition for you into that next life. I could have stroked your head, comforted you, as I did when you had a headache or a fever.

I have read that, in cases of sudden death, people need a transition period from this world to the next. Peter Marshall, the famous minister, who died of a heart attack at forty-six — the same age as you — loved, above all, to cultivate roses. After his sudden passing, he was, according to a vision of his wife, Catherine, given a grace period to work in a rose garden. Did God give you a transition period to ski a dusting of fresh powder on Colorado slopes, your favorite thing in this life? Did you come down at top speed, your Red Sleds flashing through crystalline flakes that glinted from the early morning sunlight? Our God is a loving God, and He would do that for you.

Until we meet again, my dearest husband, know that I love you more now than I did when you were with me in life. That love is immortal. Now, so are you.

Yours for eternity,
Peggy

As I read over the letter, something inside me softened. It was as if the frozen part began to thaw. In wonder, I saw that I had written, not a lamentation, but a song of praise. The letter celebrated the many great gifts my husband had given me: strength, a sense of excellence, courage, the willingness to try new things. These were gifts I still had; no one could take them from me — ever. I felt privileged, humbled. How fortunate I had been; many people never experience a fraction of the joys we had shared.

Somehow, as I poured out my heart on paper, the agonizing pain of my loss had dissipated slightly. Writing the letter was a turning point in my life as a widow. Grief, that self-centered thief, ceased to dominate my days and nights completely. I began to turn outward, toward others. After all,

I was not the only one in my group who had lost someone very dear. One of our members had lost a brother. I have a brother whom I love very much; he is still alive. One of our group had lost her fiancé at sea. They had never had a chance to share one day of married life; I had twenty-one years.

And so the letter I began in sorrow became a thanksgiving.

Today when I read it, I do not feel pain. Instead, I feel only the deep gratitude that comes from knowing how much I was loved.

Am loved.

The Endurance of Christmas

My fingers shook slightly as I unwrapped the silver-spangled star and slid it out of its tissue-paper nest. As my fingers trembled, the spangles of the star reflected the overhead light and sparkled at me.

But I didn't feel the wonder and excitement the sparkling star would have lit inside me in previous years when I unwrapped it along with the figures of my Christmas crèche. This was to be my first Christmas in a home of my own alone without my husband of twenty-one years, and I felt a hurtful wrench in the center of my chest as I thought about unwrapping the wooden figures of the crèche by myself. Since Jim had been killed, the absence of his wide grin, booming voice, and always-in-motion six-foot three-inch frame had been painfully evident in this silent house.

With no children of our own, Christmas had been a time of celebration for the two of us to share. Along with the birth of Christ, on December twenty-fifth Jim and I celebrated the deepening love we felt for each other.

I put the star down on the rug and unwrapped a hand-carved wooden sheep, part of the set that makes up the crèche. I ran my hands over the hillocks and depressions in the sheep's body that suggested curly wool, thinking as I did so that I was right not to have bought a Christmas tree. It would only have reminded me of the many times Jim and I had hiked or cross-country skied among young pines and firs, their branches decked with glistening mantles of fresh snow.

With almost ritualistic precision, I started to unwrap the other figures of the crèche, the sturdy ox and donkey and resting camel, gentle Joseph, Mary kneeling with her hands folded in prayer, a bemused shepherd boy piping a song not of this earth, and three reverent wise men cloaked in a master carver's vision of painted, gold-tinted finery. The rough-hewn brown stable sat empty on a white tablecloth above me on the card table I had set up to receive the crèche.

I couldn't do it.

In the midst of pulling the tissue from a wise man's golden crown, I stopped. My hands simply would not continue to work. I sat in the middle of the rug, the figures of the crèche mostly unwrapped, some lying on their sides, tissue-paper wads around me, pieces of straw from the stable room clinging to my skirt and sweater. *I cannot put this crèche together,* I thought. *I cannot do it without Jim. I can't look at it without him beside me.* Panic seemed to spiral up inside me with my escalating heartbeat and I was seized with a swift urge to rush out of the room. This was a terrible idea. Why had I retrieved the packed crèche from the basement? Why hadn't I just left it there with the shiny tree ornaments and strings of electric lights? Why hadn't I left Christmas to others who felt more like celebrating?

I would have to rewrap everything and carry the packed-up crèche back down to the basement.

As I looked at the disorder I had created in the middle of the room, distractedly seeing the donkey's hooves next to the folds of Mary's sunrise-colored cloak, I saw a small bundle of tissue that hadn't yet been unwrapped lying by itself to one side. I had not noticed it before; it must have fallen out of the folds of tissue wrapping another figure. Without the force of conscious will, my hands — which I thought had stopped working — picked up the tiny bundle. I unwrapped it, and found my fingers cradling the body of the baby Jesus. The wood carver had carved Him so that His left hand was folded against His body, and His right hand was stretched out — to me.

As I looked at the delicately painted face, my heartbeat slowed and the swirling thoughts of panic that had berated me left my mind. I thought of the suffering this small baby would have to endure as a man: scourging, betrayal, abandonment by those closest to Him, utter aloneness. Willingly, He had accepted it all. *Please, Jesus,* I prayed silently, *teach me to live with loneliness.* There was no sound in my old house, not even the creak of a floorboard settling itself more securely into the shape of the house.

The hand-carved wood of the infant Jesus seemed warm to the touch and almost alive in my hands. I stroked the palm of His outstretched hand with the tip of my finger. A small tear rolled down my cheek and fell on the face of the smiling baby. His smiling expression did not change. . . . Or did it? By some naturalistic alchemy — the distortion of objects seen through tears and wet lashes — the baby's smile seemed to disappear for just an instant. Was it my tear or His tear that lingered now on the baby's cheek? For a moment I could not be sure. And then my eyes cleared and the baby Jesus smiled again, a beautifully carved wooden figure — but a wooden figure, nevertheless.

I set about putting the crèche together for my home, working slowly and deliberately with calm fingers. Jim was gone. He would never again be with me to see this crèche set up in our home, and I would never get over the loss of my husband. But I could not deny Jesus a place in my home — or my heart. As I picked up the star for the top of the crèche, it shimmered in the overhead light, as it would do for all the Christmases to come.

Why Me, God?

What did Jim or I have to do with the shocking drama of his death? Who were those two uniformed detectives who had come uninvited to my front door and stepped through it into my life with their badges and their stones for words? This was what we watched on a television screen six feet away; this wasn't our life. What did we know of death certificates, pallbearers, eulogies, newspaper obituaries? Jim had a trial to prepare and argue, his booming voice filling the courtroom. We had a January ski trip to Colorado planned. I had a family dinner to cook on Sunday — a spiral-sliced ham and tomatoes from the dozen plants Jim had put in the backyard, cherry and beefsteak tomatoes. They were ripe; I really must go out and pick them. But now . . . why? They could fall and rot.

Death, the way I experienced it, was a brutal assault on the senses and the soul. It was not the joyful passage to the next life Christians have been taught to believe in. It was abrupt, messy, unfinished. It was traumatizing, at times paralyzing, to me and to many others whose lives were intertwined with Jim's. How can we find God's will in the snuffing out of productive lives in that plane crash or in another random accident? Why did Jim have to die? He was devoting his life to justice under the law. Why did Samantha Smith have to die? She had electrified the world with her trip to Communist Russia and was devoting her young life to world peace. Why did that plane crash at that particular moment in that particular wooded part of the state of Maine? Why? Why. . . ?

These were agonizing questions, questions that would not let me sleep or eat, questions that always worked their way back to me. Jim had been on a business trip; I shouldn't have let him go. So I was responsible for his death. If I had argued against the trip, then he would have stayed with me and not boarded that plane and he wouldn't have died when it crashed. Guilt came through my door after grief — that thief of all I held dear — to lodge in my heart. It wasn't rational, but it was real. The guilt weighed me down, as if I had drawn a heavy blanket of pain over myself.

Where is God in a chaotic death? Is He there at all. . . ? God is there in the people who emerge to pick up the corners of that blanket of pain, people like my church's Hank Harris, my brother, Jack, my aunt, Ann, who gave me the small green New Testament, my loving parents who came back to me from Massachusetts immediately, the friends who made their way to be by my side as soon as the clinical horror of the event became a personal story connected to someone they knew — me — not a sound bite about an anonymous plane crash on the evening news.

And God is in the process of grief, the necessary healing journey that restores a mourner gradually through soul sickness to soul health. The rawness of grief doesn't last forever, just as winter does not strip the tree limbs bare and grip the ground in its frost fingers forever. By accepting the seasons of grief — the "two steps forward, one step back" process that sometimes seems to be a timetable to nowhere — a mourner is acquiescing to that timetable, however long it takes. By living with the mourning, accepting the outstretched hands of others, and working through the grief — shock, agony, depression, and finally acceptance — healing takes place in God's own time.

There was a time when I believed that I should have been beside my husband on that plane when it slammed into the earth. That death-in-life wish did not last. It is true that there is a part of me that died with my husband on that plane; that was the Peggy-and-Jim part of me that was reserved only for him. That is the deepest part of my heart, the part only God can see now. It is true that a part of me will never be finished with the grieving, and that something — a snatch of music we danced to, a view of new snow on pine boughs — will always bring back the loss and some of the pain. It is true that I will never be the person I was before the morning of August 26, 1985.

It is also true that there is no intrinsic good in Jim's death; there is no answer to the why. But the acceptance of my husband's death has brought good: It has led to a stronger sense of identity with those who suffer and a resolve to try to share and ease their pain. I don't stay away now when death strikes in another house — a house where the doorbell will sound insistently and the phone will ring incessantly and the panoply of rituals will start over again. I go to that house; I can comfort the people there, however haltingly, because I have been comforted. I am not embarrassed by their tears or mine; they are a bond that links us, one human soul to another. Sorrow can be shared, *should* be shared. Jesus wept publicly when His friend Lazarus died; why should we behave differently?

I cannot control what happened and put things back the way they should be. I can't answer the why. I don't think any of us is meant to answer the why when a brutal accident occurs; it is beyond our knowing. Instead, we should be asking how. How can I bear this with the help of God and those who care? How can I draw closer to God in this pain? How can I use my pain to reach out to others in pain? How can I make spiritual order from this personal chaos that has plunged my soul into the pit of darkness? And finally, how can I serve God in a new way, since I will never be the same person I was before the blanket of pain descended on me?

No, I can't answer the why, for myself or for anyone else whose life is touched by tragedy. But I can choose to accept God's how of my own free will. For mourners who make this choice, I believe God will in His own time fulfill the promise to restore us to life, not death in life: "I have set before you life and death, blessing and curse; therefore choose life, that you and your descendants may live" (Deuteronomy 30:19).

What Honey Knew

The little white cat couldn't have weighed more than two and a half pounds. She sat on my parents' slate pathway and looked up toward their front door, as if she expected it to open. It was Christmas morning, a joyous blue and gold morning warming itself in early sunshine after the chilling frost of the clear night.

When my father opened the front door to get his morning paper — slimmer than usual because this was a light news day — she was sitting there on the path: two and a half pounds of white fur, green eyes, padded feet, and rosebud-pink nose. The man and the cat looked into each other's eyes: my father's deep-sea green, the cat's light yellow-green. "Why hello, honey," he said. "Do you want to come up?" And she did, climbing the circular cement steps to the front stoop on pink footpads so tiny and quiet a bird perched in the ligustrum hedge by the steps would not have startled.

The young cat looked up at my father, then rolled over on her back by the toes of his worn brown leather slippers, putting her little feet in the air so he could see the pale pink pads. My father forgot the newspaper. He forgot that the doctor had told him not to breathe in cold air. He forgot the pain he still sometimes felt along the vertical surgical scar on his chest. He bent to stroke the little cat. As he stroked her, he began to talk softly and the cat began to answer with a purr.

"Where did you come from?" he asked her. "Are you hungry? Are you cold?" For now she did seem to shiver on the cold concrete of the front stoop. My father picked the little cat up in his arms, and her body went limp and compliant against him. He held her against his shoulder and turned to go inside, newspaper forgotten.

"Can we keep her?" he asked my mother, who was standing on the hall stairs in her blue wool bathrobe. She'd come to the door, her mouth pursed and a crease between her brows because my father — who'd had a heart attack and heart surgery that fall — was taking so long to get the paper. She was about to say something about how they'd never had a cat and didn't know anything about caring for cats and how she wasn't keen on the idea of a litter box and how the cat probably belonged to someone else anyway. She was thinking that she really didn't have time for a pet. But she didn't say any of this when she looked at how the cat was curled against my father's shoulder and how my father's face looked and how his hands held the cat's white furry body.

My mother took a breath. "She is beautiful," she said. "We can keep her if we can't find her owner."

"I want to call her Honey," said my father.

And so Honey came to live with my parents, sleeping on a little bed on top of a kitchen stool and walking in the yard on a leash with a tiny red harness. If she'd ever had an owner, that person never came forward. Ads in the local paper and repeated calls to the animal shelter were pointless, as my father knew they would be. For anyone could see she was his cat. She had come, after all, on Christmas morning, that holy day when God set a new standard for gift-giving.

Honey settled in. Mainly she settled in on my father's lap, seeming to understand that he was convalescing and couldn't do very much. But Honey didn't require much. She liked to preen and lick her white coat in the morning in a spot of sunshine, and she liked an occasional scallop to vary her canned cat food. Mostly she liked to be in my father's lap. Before she leaped up lightly, she'd sit on the floor and look up at him and utter a little cat sound that ended on an up note: "P-r-r-r-t?" What it meant was, may I come up? And he'd reach for the folded yellow towel he put on his lap for her and say, "Come on up, Honey," and up she'd come.

They sat together for hours, sometimes both falling asleep, their bodies linked by their warmth and the gentle harmony of their breathing. My mother called Honey my father's nurse. But she knew Honey was better than any human nurse, for the little white cat offered something nurses didn't seem to provide. Whatever it was, it worked, because my father healed.

Honey and I got to know each other better when I ghost-walked back to my parents' house for a while after the death of my husband Jim in a plane crash. I spent time on my parents' flowered love seat, exhausted by shock and grief, hardly able to lift my arm. Now Honey had more immediate work to do. She came and sat at the base of the love seat and looked up at me, hoping I'd notice her through the gray gauze of grief that wrapped me like a mummy. "P-r-r-r-t?" she asked in her little cat voice. I looked down and motioned her up, my arm seeming to move in slow motion, and patted my stomach. It was such an effort to move that arm.

But it was all she needed. Up she came, a mature cat now but still tiny; she weighed no more than six pounds. Honey settled her body onto mine. Then she looked into my brown eyes with her yellow-green ones. Her face was so close that I could see how her eyes had depth and pinpoints of light, like faceted jewels. Her eyes were speaking to me in a cat language known just to her.

"What?" I asked her.

She started to purr and settled herself more securely against my body. "Let me, let me, let me, let me," her purr seemed to say.

And so I did let her: I let her sit with me and purr and comfort me in a way many people outside my family and circle of friends seemed unable to do. For so many of them asked questions. I could not answer the questions, as if the blow that had caused the cleavage of my heart had also lopped off my tongue. So many of the people talked *at* me. I could not catch their words and respond, as an outfielder would have caught baseballs and thrown them back to home plate.

Honey asked no questions. She didn't talk at me. Her purr did not demand a response. She wanted only to snuggle against me and be there with me. With the vibrations of Honey's purring and her warmth against me, day after day, I came to feel less mummified by the winding sheet of grief.

When I left my parents' house to live on my own, Honey resumed her place on the old folded yellow towel on my father's lap, faded now from many washings and always covered with little white hairs. Honey stayed on my father's lap as much as she could until she died at the age of twenty, her body made thin and gaunt by kidney disease and a cancer that put a bleeding growth on one ear. But Honey's yellow-green eyes stayed bright like faceted gems, and her coat was still as white as talc.

Like her coming, Honey's going was a special time on the church calendar, as if she knew about the significance of these things. Honey died at Easter, a time when both my father and I were breathing in the scent of potted lilies and hyacinths and looking at the jonquils waving their yellow tops outside and the buds on the red maples and the way the grass greened and sprouted in clumps and the wild onion tops spiked the backyard.

My father's heart was beating strongly, helped by medication and love. My winding sheet of grief was gone, the stripping Honey started completed by my family and the gentle words of people in my life who never asked questions or talked at me.

Honey was cremated by her longtime veterinarian, a man with large, deft, kind hands who had looked into Honey's yellow-green eyes and my father's deep-sea ones and who understood the tears people wept for beloved animals. My father scattered Honey's ashes at the base of a young cherry tree in his front yard. When the cherry tree blooms, as it does every spring, the petals of its delicate blossoms are as white as talc. They are as white as Honey's fur — except for a tinge of pink as pale as the pads of her little feet.

Unshuttering the Soul

When does the winter heart begin to thaw? When does the tiniest of seeds in a barren soil find enough nourishment to germinate?

There is a time, at first undetected as a mourner passes through the seasons of grief, when the first green shoot of hope begins to grow. There is a time when trust, betrayed and battered, sends forth a new green shoot to grow beside hope.

The soul's last defense is shutting down to avoid more pain. Like the closed-in turtle or the slammed-tight clam, the shuttered soul sends its message: Please don't touch. And then some time, at some point in God's own time, a hand reaches out across a restaurant table and I want to take that hand. It is not Jim's hand. It is smaller, adept at using hammers and screwdrivers. It is a hand that has caressed another woman's face, the face of a beloved dead wife. This woman, Patricia, was blond, not dark-haired like me. It is a hand that has held the bow of a violin, a hand belonging to a man who was once the child of a Belgian mother who came from a family of musicians and painters.

This man's name is Rudy, not Jim: Rudolf Alfonse Ruda, a name with the sense of old Europe about its letters, a name that should be written in script. It is a name unlike James Coburn Eastman, whose sounds are rooted in Colonial America and should be printed in block letters. Rudy is a businessman and a photographer, not a lawyer.

Is healing making peace with our memories? If we make peace with them, maybe they won't wound us anymore. If we can blunt the knife edges, maybe we can take away the power to hurt. God, the great healer, guides this blunting process. At first the memories cut so deeply we believe we will die from the pain. The hurt is greater because the one we loved most deeply did the cutting. The reasoning is skewed, but it is real: Jim, if you loved me so much, how could you have hurt me so deeply? And then the transference to God: God, if You love me much, how could You have betrayed me so completely? How could You have taken from me the one life more precious than my own? The life I want more than anything but You?

Through God's gentle blunting the hurt lessens. Rudy and I — brought together out of our pain in a church bereavement group — talk about this. Early on in my pain, I tell him I was born to suffer. He disagrees, stops my words with his. "God doesn't want that for you," he says. "He has something else for you." So what God wants, we conclude, is to leave us the best parts of our memories, the parts that don't cut like knife wounds: Jim turning to look back at me on a wooded hiking trail, telling me to watch out for that rock, that one just there near my left foot; Patricia bending over her whimpering first child, a dark-haired daughter named Carrie, to soothe her, kiss her soft cheek, and coax the little pixie face into a dimpled smile.

But what of the memories we don't have, the ones that were stolen from us? What do we do with our regrets about the memories that never were? The mountain slope of fresh powder not skied with Jim, the infant grandson Patricia didn't live to see? Rudy and I decide they are like half-painted dreams we must give back to God, the master painter, unfinished. They are the parts of us that might have been, the parts we would have chosen for ourselves, had our feet not been set on other paths.

"It won't ever be the same," says a member of our bereavement group. No, it won't. I am not the person I was. Rudy is not the person he was. The Jim-and-Peggy part of me is gone. The Patricia-and-Rudy part of Rudy is gone. But if I unshutter my soul, just a little bit at first, I may find that a new and different person is struggling to come out. Will that wounded person be better? Will I like her? Can I live with her? And more: Could there . . . would there . . . ever be a Rudy-and-Peggy part?

Sitting in that bereavement group I don't know the answers, and so I bargain childishly with God: If You want me to serve You, You have to bring me out of the pit and give me something to replace what I lost. But this is a foolish request, an impertinent request, and I see it immediately: God doesn't *have* to do anything. He doesn't have to give me anything. He is not a bargainer. His ways are not our ways; we can only catch faint firefly glimmers of His ways in the heavy summer darkness, never the fully illuminated design of His creation.

To love again must be part of that illuminated design

only He can see. That is why I feel these nudges toward a man who is not Jim, never could be. A man whose name should be written in script, not block letters. God doesn't intend us to live with shuttered souls. He sent Jesus, the greatest wooer of shuttered souls, to show us we don't have to live without love.

A winter heart can thaw. A tiny seed can germinate and grow. A person can grow and change into someone who was not born to suffer, a person who can laugh at a joke told in good faith, taste the garlic in spaghetti sauce not made for Jim, see the dew on a pale yellow rosebud, feel a rush of joy at the call of a cardinal. A person who can stretch out a hand to a new hand, a good hand, not Jim's hand, and take it in trust. A person who can stand before God and others at an altar and once more say "I do."

Love is the eternal now, here, right this minute. It is not one place. It is not one moment in time. It is not one person. It does not die when that one person dies. It is with us always, to the end of the ages. It is how we were meant to live.

Alice's Bear

My ten-year-old niece, Alice, was bent over her kitchen table, putting the last touches of paint on a present for Rudy, who was hospitalized with cancer. As I watched Alice's fingers working on the small clay bear — so much concentration and patience for a ten-year-old — I thought how unfair it was that she should have to make this get-well present at all.

Rudy and Alice and I should be on a soccer field, Alice running hard with her thick dark-gold hair flying out behind her as we cheered her down toward the goal. Alice and Rudy and Alice's twelve-year-old brother, Christopher, and I should be walking on the shore, the children gathering conch and slipper shells while Rudy and I, walking hand in hand, let the frothy little waves that advanced and receded lap at our toes.

But Rudy, my beloved second husband, Rudy who had shared my tears and my grief, Rudy who had helped my winter heart to thaw, was in a hospital bed with tubes in his arm. The hospital was a foreign place to me, a place of disinfectant and forced cheerfulness and briskness, and its impact was felt most vividly in images I wished I had not stored in my mind to replay.

Image: I am standing at the elevators that feed 5 East, the chemotherapy floor, with Rudy's older daughter, Carrie. We have caught Dr. S. in flight as he heads to a medical conference (do they ever sit down, these doctors?).

Dr. S. says, "He had to have emergency radiation because the tumor was pressing on key nerves."

Carrie asks a question; I am stunned into silence by the matter-of-fact clinical language that brings bad news and more bad news, nothing but bad news.

"It's a bad cancer," Dr. S. tells Carrie.

In a small voice I ask, "Isn't there anything else? Any experimental treatment?"

Dr. S. shakes his head, no. It's no, no, and no. He talks about the chemotherapy drugs, cisplatin and VP-16.

Another image comes to me, an image from a few months before. Rudy is complaining of pain in his chest. I want to hold him, to put my hands on his chest and make the pain go away. I feel somehow responsible for this pain. God gave Rudy to me, and somehow I must heal him and make him whole. I must do something to stop this pain, but I feel isolated with it. How do I fight it? What tools do I use? His eyes hurt. I can see the pain in those eyes I love. Before we married, Rudy said, "There's more to love than kisses." Yes, much more, but where will I find the more he needs? The doctors don't have it, so I must be the one to find the something more for him.

Now I hug Alice and say, "Alice, you're a wonderfully kind and thoughtful girl to work so hard on this bear; I know the bear will make Rudy feel much better. I'll put it on his hospital windowsill." And then I make my feet carry me to the car, which will carry me to the hospital where they don't seem to be able to do much for my husband.

That night, back in my empty house in a bed without Rudy, I couldn't fall asleep. The thought of losing him was there somewhere, buried, but I wouldn't let it surface. I would not let myself believe that God would put me through the long process of grief again. It couldn't be. Then, about 4:00 A.M., I sat straight up in bed with a start. Where was Alice's bear?

Oh, no, I thought, as I suddenly remembered placing the bear on the hood of my car while I put some rubber-band-bundled get-well cards and wrapped packages in the car for Rudy. *How could I have been so stupid?* I berated myself. I was such a slow and cautious driver that people behind me often honked, but no doubt the hand-painted bear had fallen off somewhere on the short drive to the hospital and was now in shards. I would never find the little clay bear on the road; even if I did, I couldn't put him back together. *Should I go look for the pieces of the bear tomorrow?*

I tossed from one side to the other for most of the night on the empty bed that should have had Rudy in it, worrying about what I would say to Alice, worrying about what I would tell Rudy and kicking myself mentally for being so careless with a child's trust. Finally, I stopped tossing and said a simple prayer: "Lord, I know it's impossible, but You're the God of the impossible. This might seem like a very small request, but it's not small to me. Please let Alice's bear be on the hood of my car when I get up tomorrow." As I prayed, I felt a strong sense of relief that I could share my worry with God. I wasn't alone in my house with this, and I no longer felt so stupid. I fell asleep saying silently, "Lord of the impossible. . . ."

I hardly dared look at the car that morning when I opened my front door clothed in my old red plaid bathrobe, but I had to make myself do it. As I looked, I gasped. There, lying on the hood of my aging white Buick was the little bear with a smile on his face and "I LOVE YOU" printed in Alice's ten-year-old hand on his tummy. I breathed a prayer of thanksgiving as I picked up the little bear and held him in my hand, thanksgiving because in this time of worry over big things that might not be able to be fixed, God had given me a gift of mercy over something small that mattered.

Comfort from Beyond the Grave

When Rudy died of cancer on October 13, 1994, in the Washington Home Hospice, I was so angry at God I could not make my feet take me through the large brown double doors of my church. It was a church of death; the memorial services for both of the men I loved had been held there, two husbands in nine years. I couldn't make my feet go there anymore and feel the constant dull pain in my insides, or experience the bouts of crying that came unbidden.

Why had God brought Rudy and me together in our church bereavement group only to snatch him from me? Back then, my church had seemed a place of refuge, a place of healing. Why had God drawn us to each other on this sacred ground after tragedy, blunted our pain, and helped us love again only to end our happy four-year marriage so abruptly? Irrationally, I thought somehow the church must be to blame. It had hurt me too much. I could not sit in that church alone in a pew without my husband. Without which husband? Rudy? Jim? *God, couldn't You have left me one of them? Did You have to take them both?* As I thought of this double tragedy, a fresh wave of grief washed over me, and I became prey to self-pity.

One Sunday after purposely missing church — again — I wandered through the rooms of my empty house aimlessly, turning my head away from Rudy's favorite reclining armchair, the one next to the shelf with his folded wire-rimmed reading glasses. I tried not to look at the mail stacked on the dining room table because I knew some of the letters would ask for death certificates (again) and some of it would be from people who didn't know he was dead. I would have to tell them. The dull ache in the pit of my stomach seemed to get worse, and I felt the tears pricking my eyelids. Again.

I went up the stairs and stood in Rudy's study, looking at the empty desk chair, the books he would never open again, the photos of us on the walls. The tears flowed down my cheeks as I looked at our honeymoon photo, taken in a New York hotel. He looked so tall and strong in his dark suit, standing behind my chair. He looked so loving and protective. I swallowed, then said aloud, "Rudy, you've got to help me." It seemed the cruelest of ironies: The one person in the world who could have helped me with this grief was the one who had caused it.

As I stood in the empty study, a message imprinted itself on my brain: "Open the file cabinet." The message was so vivid I turned my head as if toward a voice, but I was alone in the room. I went to his file cabinet, something I had never done: It was private. I knew I would have to get to these papers eventually, but I had been putting it off. The empty study only deepened my sense of loss. I heard the voice again, more insistent this time: "Open the top drawer."

I drew open the heavy file drawer hesitantly, wondering if I should be doing this right now. I felt like a trespasser. I glanced quickly at the titles on some of the file folders: auto, children, medical, Patricia, travel. . . . Then my eyes were drawn back to a file folder marked "grief/faith." I put my hand out to touch it, then drew it back. This was more than personal; it was sacred. It would have things in it he had written when his wife Patricia died. I shouldn't be looking here.

The voice was stronger now, more insistent: "Open it." I took the file out quickly and walked into our bedroom, sitting on the edge of our queen-size bed. The one I hadn't slept in since he died, using the twin bed in the tiny guest room. Rudy's medications were still lined up on the side table; his worn suede slippers were still by the right side of the bed, the side where he had always slept, the one with the slight depression where his six-foot frame had rested.

I opened the file, almost afraid to touch its contents. Carefully, as if touching very old parchment, I leafed through newspaper clippings on coping with grief, sympathy cards received at the time of Patricia's death, a personal letter of condolence to Rudy from our pastor. Then I came to a piece of paper with words written in his handwriting; the handwriting was so familiar I wanted to clutch the lined piece of notepaper to my heart. But I was afraid to look. This wasn't written to me or for me. It wasn't meant for me at all.

"Read it." That voice in my head again.

I started reading, feeling that I was violating a sacred trust, wanting to put the piece of paper down and put the file away in its drawer. Rudy's drawer. Rudy's file cabinet. Rudy's study.

"Growth through creative suffering," I read. "Spiritual pain equals dying. Help us to know in our hearts that Your sustaining power is there for the taking." Some of the words were crossed out and replaced with others, as if he had worked on this for a while.

"Your sustaining power is there for the taking." As I read the words written in Rudy's handwriting, it seemed a kind of prayer he had brought out of his pain, and I could almost see him kneeling beside me in church. As I continued to read his words, the dull ache in my stomach began to lessen. It was almost as if he were sitting there on the edge of the bed beside me, talking to me and praying with me in that caring voice I had come to rely on in our marriage for my daily strength.

"Give us the power to reach out in the darker hours," I read. "Give us the faith to trust that there will be a new, bright day. You will not leave me comfortless. Amen."

"Not leave me comfortless." How was it that, like me, Rudy had also been led to rely on Jesus' promise in John 14:18? The promise marked by my aunt Ann's squiggly pencil line in the small green New Testament she had pressed into my hands after Jim died. The promise Rudy had clung to after Patricia died. I thought of Rudy reading the same passage in his Bible after his wife's car accident. I wondered if his tears had fallen on the pages of his Bible, marking this page in John's Gospel just as surely as my aunt's squiggly pencil mark. I wondered if he had read this passage over and over, as I had. I thought of how he had helped me work through my grief when Jim died, as I had helped him work through his grief over Patricia's death.

I thought of what Rudy would say to me, if he could come and sit on the bed next to me. I pictured him holding me in his arms, comforting me. Reading what he had written brought me closer to him. Somehow, I didn't feel so abandoned now. For the first time since I had lost him a month before, I began to believe that Rudy's love was still with me. And that his loving presence would stay with me.

I put the lined piece of paper with his handwritten message carefully back in the file folder and replaced it in its drawer where I had been directed to find it. Next Sunday, I would go back to church.

Loneliness-Not-Named-Right

It is hard to know when grief becomes something else, something with less power to cleave, something that leaves us less desperate and stricken. There is an imperceptible slide through the days from hurting all over — pain with no antidote — to something else. For want of a more specific word to describe this dulling of pain, we choose the word "loneliness."

"Solitude" will not do, for it can be a good friend, drawing us nearer the divine around us and the divine within us. Loneliness — which connotes desolation, the state of being bereft, sadness from being alone, and an absence of chosen human company — will have to do for this between-time from grief to . . . what? I don't know, for although I have walked this mountain journey of the soul twice, the paths are different and I have neither map nor compass. Maybe there is nothing after the between-time. Maybe this between-time is the final time. Maybe it is all I will ever know.

What is the color of this state we call loneliness because we lack a more precise term? Does it have a scent? How to take its measure? Is it catching? What is its shape? Does it have depth? Weight? Does it displace space?

If it has a color, it must certainly be gray, hue of mourning doves and used shrouds. What does it resemble, this state with the imprecise name: an unwelcome guest? Illness? A demanding intruder? A turncoat friend? Its presence is like that of an illness, insistent, constant, wanting in. It is surely a close cousin of yearning, for there is a leaning toward, not a cavernous emptiness.

Leaning toward what? The absence of knowing what is part of the grayness, but the color gray can lighten or darken. There is, maybe, light somewhere in here, light that one could befriend. For even in illness there are times when the fever drops a few degrees or the pain abates, and in those times the illness is almost a friend.

If it sticks around long enough, this loneliness-not-named-right will become part of the paint on the walls, the upholstery on the chairs. It will merge into the steam from the bathwater, make itself part of the scent of strong coffee emanating from the percolator. It will put itself on with my

clothes when I rise, drag itself into the car to go grocery shopping, lagging as my feet lag with these chores. I feel it around
me as I get into bed at night, so much a part of the blanket
that the familiar blue woolliness settles with a weight not
entirely its own.

*If I put you on and sip you and let you walk the shopping
aisles with my cart and sleep beside me, can I make a friend of
you? If not a friend, at least an acquaintance worth an occasional "hello"? No, not an acquaintance, for acquaintances are
not there all the time the way you are. Not so intimately present.*

There is something importunate in this insistent intimacy.
I don't want you, but you come in anyway. If I told you to go
you wouldn't, so I don't. What I am afraid of is that you will do
more than put yourself on with my clothes. I am afraid you
will find a way inside my skin, working your way in like chiggers, those tiny six-legged predators of summer that feast on
blood just under the skin of bare legs. If you get inside me,
really inside me, how will I ever get you out? Chiggers eventually die, sated, but your leaning-toward yearning seems too
strong to be sated. What would you feed on, deep inside me?
Snapshots from Jim-dreams or Rudy-dreams I had placed
under plastic for safekeeping?

Click, snap: Jim is at the tiller of the *Windsong,* his
rumpled brimmed sailing hat with plaid band pulled down to
the tops of the sunglasses that rest on his straight nose, a
strand of blond hair blowing free of the hat, a smile curving
his lips up just before they part, slouchy tee shirt settling in
folds around his waist where those faded brown bathing
trunks begin.

Click, snap: Jim is on his Red Sled skis ahead of me,
taking the turns as tightly as he can considering how long
and unforgiving these stiff skis are, powder sprays spewing
out with each turn, upper body hunched forward with effort,
yellow down-filled jacket straining at the shoulders where the
sleeves begin, head bobbing a little in its green wool stocking
cap with white band.

Click, snap: Jim is pacing with the long steps I could
never keep up with on the gold rug in the living room, white
shirttail escaping from his belt, a yellow legal pad in his left
hand, a plastic ballpoint pen with a chewed end in his right.
He stops, rests the pad on the mantelpiece askew (for the

mantel is too narrow to serve as his desk), and writes something down quickly with the chewed-end pen, then he is off pacing again . . . and thinking . . . and pacing.

Click, snap: I am holding a glass of lemonade for Rudy in the garage with its mixed scent of gasoline and turpentine; Rudy is lying on his back under his old slate-blue Mercedes convertible, checking out the extent of the rust he knows will call for hours of his time. He strokes its underside gently, feeling the metal of the disabled sports car with hands used to wielding tools as carefully as a surgeon uses his scalpels, calculating the extent of treatment needed to restore this car to a loving companion of the open road.

Click, snap: Rudy is sitting beside me in church in his brown-striped suit, holding the prayer book out carefully in front of us with his dexterous hands that can play the violin as well as wield a power sander, holding the book more on my side than his so he can be sure I will be able to see the words. He moves a little closer, his side touching mine, turns his head and smiles.

Click, snap: Rudy and I are walking a tree-lined path in Quiet Waters Park, his camera on its strap bumping and nudging his chest as he walks. He stops in front of a young dogwood tree, its leaves flaming with the red of an early autumn, and circles the tree, marking the sunlight from different angles, looking for the position he wants. He finds it, stooping and shooting the young tree so its leaves are backlit, veins illuminated, some leaves shadowed by others in patchwork patterns, branches of different thicknesses reaching upward toward the light and sometimes catching that light so their darkness is glow-coated on top.

If in feeding on these Jim-reveries and Rudy-memories this loneliness-not-named-right can bring them back to me with the immediacy of sail-billowing wind, spraying snow, the scent of gasoline and turpentine, the words on the page of a prayer book ("Almighty God, Father of all mercies"), and the light on a red dogwood leaf, why should I try to make the yearning leave me?

A Shore So Far

Our women's book club of thirteen had splurged for our twenty-fifth anniversary: We'd rented a beach house on a stretch of North Carolina's sparsely populated Outer Banks for a September weekend during the off-season.

The tourists were gone; the college students were back in class; the sand and water were still warm. We'd seen photos of the house in a realtor's brochure and fallen in love. As much a support group as a book-reading club, the thirteen of us would talk and share. Carol and Virginia and I had recently lost spouses; Mary had been through a hurtful divorce. Other book club members had sick and elderly parents.

The rules were simple: no men allowed, bring food to share, a bathing suit, and your own sheets and towels. Virginia would make us some of her gourmet pasta salads with vinaigrette dressing; Carol would tell us about her latest lion jewelry designs; Jill would bring her laptop; Marilyn would shoot candid photos; and Mary would stretch out on a beach towel and let the sun soak into her caramel-colored arms and legs. Jane, the athletic, capable mother of five, would jog on the sand, find the nearest church to attend on Sunday, and invite us all to come. It was Jane — five years older than I — who'd brought me into this nurturing book club, Jane who'd taught me to ski, Jane who'd come when my husband Jim was killed.

As for me, I wanted to commune with the waves the Atlantic Ocean sent rolling onto that long stretch of open, sandy shore. I wanted the ocean's timelessness; I wanted its healing. I felt its tug on my bruised soul, a tug as seductive as the waves of grief that sometimes rolled over me, pulling me back to the past. We'd been warned about the undertow off the Outer Banks; "Just don't go too far out," a shopkeeper told us when we'd stopped for milk and eggs. "Remember, there're no lifeguards this time of year," the realtor had said when we'd picked up the key. "Be careful."

But somehow we didn't think about that when we saw the house: bleached gray wood and glass on stilts, a see-through box that looked as if it might take off and rise up to meet the sky. It was right on the beach, just a quick run in bare feet on hot sand to the waves. "Oh-h-h," we breathed out together, and the collective sigh of pleasure mingled with the lightest of September sea breezes.

The next morning we rose to the smell of Virginia's fresh-brewed hazelnut coffee and put on our bathing suits. We slathered sunscreen lotion on one another's backs, gathered up straw hats and sunglasses, and picked up towels, two beach umbrellas, an ice chest, and books, our cache of light beach reading. Jane was already up and out jogging.

"Who's going in?" I asked, the olive-colored sea calling its invitation as the waves receded and crashed, receded and crashed. "I will," said Carol, Jill, and Virginia. We ran like children down to the surf, glad to be shedding burdens that belonged to adults as we took off our wide-brimmed hats and sunglasses.

A wave came rolling in and we all jumped, water spraying our faces. We waded in farther, until we were just past the waves' breaking point. Here we could touch bottom and feel the swells around us, rising and falling, rising and falling. . . .

"It's so . . . womblike," I said. This was what I wanted: the gentle, healing touch of water.

I could feel the bottom and see Jill's face as I moved my arms back and forth. But then suddenly — I couldn't anymore. I dog-paddled rapidly, and then tried to put my foot down. Nothing. Where was Jill? My mouth and nose went under and I dog-paddled harder, spluttering. Never a strong swimmer, I felt panic rising up in me faster than anger. Now there was no one near me. Where had they gone?

Now the waves were tugging me out with them; this must be what they meant by the Outer Banks undertow. Breathing hard, I tried to do a crawl toward the shore, but the harder I worked my arms the farther out I seemed to go. My heart was pounding now as I saw my book club friends on the shore under the two beach umbrellas — one green-and-white striped, one with orange and yellow daisies — the scene an impressionist painter's vivid dots of color.

I tried to yell, but water rushed into my mouth and no sound came out, and my friends and the umbrellas were getting smaller . . . I was tiring. *Got to get to shore . . . legs so weak . . . kick . . . don't want to kick . . . arms too heavy . . . too heavy to lift. . . .*

A feather drifted by my nose. How easily it rode the waves. *Maybe if I just . . . turned . . . and kicked down . . . I could roll onto my back and float. . . .* Now it didn't take so much energy.

As I looked up, I saw bits of cloud fluff drifting by — so small in the sky, like me in the water. A gull soared, then coasted. *Was it the gull who'd lost a feather?* I wondered idly. Then I realized my heart was no longer pounding and I was no longer struggling, just floating and floating. . . .

A sense of peace settled over me as I floated on the swells. *I'm so tired, Lord, so tired of fighting the undertow and the waves of grief. . . . Is this the time for me to come to You, Lord? Floating on the swells of Your ocean? Take me home, then. . . . I wish I could tell them how easy it is . . . just like a drifting feather. . . .*

"Peggy," I heard someone say near my head. *Jane?* I wanted to say, but I only thought it in my head. Where did Jane — the strongest swimmer of us all — come from? She hadn't gone into the water with us; she'd been out jogging. Maybe my life was passing in front of me before I died.

An image of Jane came unbidden to my mind: Jane skiing slowly down a slope of sun-washed hardpack in a navy blue jacket and jeans, legs planted firmly in a snow plow with front ski tips together. I, the beginner, was following behind, an ungainly stork with tight and aching leg muscles. Jane lifted a ski pole, turned her head and her blue eyes to me, smiled, and said, "That's it, you're doing great."

Jane turned toward me in the swells of water. "Swim alongside the shore," she commanded. I rolled onto my stomach, tried to lift my heavy left arm. "That's it, you're doing great," she said. Now I could see her face: not an image, real. "Don't try to swim against the current," she said. "Swim along behind me." Another image came: Jane sitting by me after Jim died, not saying anything, just there beside me.

Suddenly, looking at Jane's white neck and strong, muscled arms working in front of me, I didn't want to drift out like that feather. I wanted to fight my way back to shore, to follow Jane, to sit under the bright beach umbrellas and slather on sunscreen and eat Virginia's pasta salad. . . . *Not the right time, Lord. Please, give me strength to get back.* Maybe I could make my legs kick . . . aching muscles . . . *lift the right arm . . . kick. . . .* Now I didn't think about the aching muscles and I felt new strength in my arms. I didn't think about how far out we were; I followed Jane, swimming right behind her as I had followed her down that ski slope, working my way back.

Far down the shoreline from the two beach umbrellas my feet touched sand beside Jane and I breast-stroked with my last ounce of strength to get in closer to shore; now I let the waves take me in, not out. Before my legs finally gave way and I fell onto the sand on my knees — dripping sea water and tears — Jane said, breathing hard, "You did great."

I wanted to answer: words tumbling out saying thank you for stopping the undertow, thank you for the skiing, thank you for being there when Jim died, thank you for the book club, thank you for the sand under my feet. . . .

But I had no breath to say it. And I was going to ask, when I had breath, "Who sent you out after me?" But I didn't, because both Jane and I knew.

Strong to Save

It is April 23, 1995. Ginny and I, both widows, stand beside each other in church trying to sing the hymn "Eternal Father, Strong to Save," around the lumps in our throats. *Eternal Father, strong to save, whose arm hath bound the restless wave. . . .*

Ginny's voice quavers. I try to wipe a tear as it travels down my cheek and hold my hymnal at the same time . . . *who bidd'st the mighty ocean deep its own appointed limits keep: O hear us when we cry to thee for those in peril on the sea.* I swipe at another tear. *Most Holy Spirit, who didst brood upon the chaos dark and rude, and bid its angry tumult cease, and give, for wild confusion, peace: O hear us when we cry to thee for those in peril on the sea.*

When the hymn is over, I put the hymnal down with a hand that trembles. I am thinking of Ginny's husband, Jack, whom I never knew; Jack, blond and laughing and strong, perished on this day in a shipboard explosion in 1945. I am also thinking of my father, who is standing next to me on the other side, and of my two dead husbands, Jim — blond and laughing and strong — who served as an Army officer; and Rudy — dark and laughing and strong — who was a Marine officer. Ginny and I are separated in age by nearly three decades; but as we stand together in this small church, the interwoven threads of our lives hold us together as tightly as the words of the Scriptures we say in unison.

April 23, 1945. The news account is terse: "Some 49 officers and men were lost and 13 others survived when a mysterious explosion ripped apart a World War I type navy patrol boat three miles off Cape Elizabeth (Maine). . . . Officials did not ascertain immediately whether the blast was caused by enemy action, a drifting mine, or defective mechanism or armament on the vessel. The survivors, who called themselves 'The Lucky Thirteen,' included only one of the ship's six officers. The sinking of the [615-ton] U.S.S. PE-56 [Eagle patrol boat] was believed to have caused the heaviest loss of life among navy personnel serving on the New England coast in the present war." Ginny's husband, Jack, was not the one officer of the Lucky Thirteen.

Jack was my father's executive officer when my father was captain of the PE-56. Had my father not requested a transfer to the Pacific to be closer to enemy action in World War II shortly before the shipboard explosion, he might have been one of the forty-nine men who died when the ship sank. I knew this irony caused my father deep pain; I also knew Ginny had said if he'd still been captain when the explosion hit, the ship would have been saved. I'd heard the stories until they'd achieved the burnished aura of myth: how I, a toddler, had seen my mother's stricken face when she received the letter from Ginny's brother telling her Jack had been lost at sea, and how I'd said, "What's the matter, Mommy, did something happen to Daddy's ship?" She had uttered not one word when she read the letter; how had I been able to read my mother's face? Fifty years later, they still wondered at it.

I'd heard how Ginny, a young bride, had seen my mother pushing me in a stroller in Key West, Florida, before she'd even known who we were, and how she'd said she'd like to get to know us. I'd heard how Jack had become my father's closest friend as well as his executive officer; they shared more than the same first name. I knew Ginny had driven north up Route 1 with my pregnant mother and me from Key West to Portland, Maine, as both women followed the Eagle patrol boat 56 up the coast. I'd heard the story of how Ginny, in shock, called her brother in Baltimore, Maryland, when she got the news in Portland about her husband from the Navy and her brother said on the crackling telephone over the long miles between them, "Hold on, Ginny, it might be a mistake. Stay right there; I'm coming up." I'd heard about how much in love Ginny and Jack were, and how he'd vowed to work to make his marriage perfect if he could (because his own parents bickered), about how he'd held her in his arms, bending his blond head to her dark one, and kissed her and told her not to worry, he'd be coming back. Ginny, with a face as fragile as a flower's and a lithe body as small as a girl's, had believed him because she wanted so much to believe.

But he didn't come back because he wasn't the one officer of the Lucky Thirteen.

I knew that through the years the intertwined threads holding Ginny and my parents together had grown tighter: that she'd visited them on vacation in Massachusetts; that they'd driven to the Maryland farm to visit her after she'd remarried, taking her vows with a man she'd known in high school; that they kept up with each other not only through visits and phone calls but through talking with mutual friends, who happened to be the parents of a boy I knew in high school. I knew they still chuckled together over the story of going to a restaurant — the three couples with their intertwined lives — and how my father, who insisted on paying the bill, reached into his back pocket for his wallet and discovered it wasn't there. Without hesitation, the father of my classmate pulled out his money to pay. They still laughed at the look on my father's face that night when he realized he'd forgotten his wallet.

Now Ginny and my father and mother and I walk up to the altar of this small church to receive the holy Eucharist in memory of the men who died on a ship that sank on April 23, 1945. Before this altar, I say a prayer of thanksgiving for my father's life, and for the fact that God spared him so he could be standing in church with us today. I say prayers of thanks for the life of Ginny's husband Jack, whom I never knew. I say prayers for the lives of my husbands Jim and Rudy, and for Ginny's kind second husband, Elliott. The words of the Psalm for this day seem to have been chosen for all these beloved and honorable men: "Open to me the gates of righteousness, / that I may enter through them and give thanks to the LORD" (Psalm 118:19).

✻ ✻ ✻

It is an April day in 1997. Ginny and I are sitting in a small neighborhood luncheonette, the kind where you pour your own coffee into disposable plastic cups that sit in plastic holders. The luncheonette is in a shopping center across the street from the church where two years ago we honored the men who died on the U.S.S. PE-56 on April 23, 1945. Ginny and I have become even closer friends, and we like to meet in this self-service luncheonette that caters to retirees and workingmen. I am no longer the little girl with curls being pushed by her mother in a stroller in wartime Key West. I, like Ginny, have become a childless widow.

I fetch Ginny's coffee, black, and sit down at the Formica-top table that separates us by three feet and unites us across nearly three decades and more than fifty years. Ginny puts a

53

stapled stack of about ten pages down on the table. I see that these pages are typed on a manual typewriter.

"Peggy," she says, "I want you to have these."

I hold them in my hands, seeing that the pages are titled "So Lovingly Remembered." They are dedicated to Ginny's husband, Jack, lieutenant, U.S.N.R. On the title page is typed "He gave his life for his country, April 23, 1945," and "A country can live only as long as she has men who are ready to die for her." And, "This collection of poems is written in memory of my son, Jack. I hope they will strike a chord in the hearts of other mothers who have lost a son." (*And widows who have lost a husband*, I think.)

Ginny sips her coffee quietly. I glance through these poems, leafing through more than fifty years.

I see that Jack's mother — a woman long dead whom I never knew — has written poems from her heart. I see that the poems are for all of us, all of us women who have lost their men, whether in battle or not. In "Men Like You," Jack's mother has written:

> When I see the one you left, so bereft of all joy in life,
> And know my own ache of longing for you —
> How can I say other than "No"?
> And when I see the world as it is today,
> Still more do I protest — No!
> The cost was priceless, and we who have accepted the
> sacrifice
> Have proven ourselves less than worthy.

The cry of an anguished woman unused to expressing herself in verse rises with the words of these poems. And yet there is so much more than anguish. There is joy and pride, too. Jack's mother has written:

> It was such fun that day, you were so handsome in your
> uniform,
> And Ginny always lovely;
> I felt great pride in both of you; she wanted an ice-cream
> cone,
> And how you teased her!
> We sat on the bank of the little pond, throwing stones. . . .

As we talked of all those days gone by
You seeing things so wisely in retrospect.
I remember the joy I felt in your maturity.
I knew then that no matter what crisis you would be called
    to face,
You would meet it the right way.
Little could I know how soon that time would come.

But there is much more for us in these poems even than anguish, joy, and pride, I see. Jack's mother has not let her anger and her grief overwhelm her. She has not turned her back on God. She has not become embittered. In these poems of a mother who lost her son in World War II there is a quiet acceptance and an affirmation of faith in One who is always strong to save. And there is a plea that God will come to comfort her when she calls on Him, and the implied assurance that He will. Jack's mother has written:

I know you were there, God, to comfort him
There to take his hand and lift him from the cold angry
    waters
To your loving heart.
I know your love was so great, he forgot his grief and
    loneliness
Leaving us whom he loved so dearly. . . .
So I find respite in my grief and loneliness,
Knowing he is with You whose love is beyond our
    understanding.
Merciful God, let me feel You here beside me in my sorrow;
Grant me a sense of his nearness, and a quiet peace,
Knowing no harm nor pain can touch him now.

I raise my eyes from these pages written by Jack's mother after World War II and look across the Formica-top table and into Ginny's hazel eyes. I see the eyes of a young bride who loved to eat ice-cream cones her husband bought for her and curl into his arms at night when they went to bed together. Looking through these eyes, I see other eyes. I see the eyes of a teenaged girl weeping at the casket of the older brother who once held out his hand so she could climb to their planked tree house in a leafy oak; I see the eyes of a mother cradling her whimpering newborn son in her arms and wishing she could keep him safe there forever. I see the eyes of a white-haired woman in a long black dress placing a bouquet of fragrant white lilies by a gravestone that has been there long enough to settle into earth that has yielded to its weight, the dirt sighing and shifting around the stone.

As I look into Ginny's eyes, it seems I am looking across more than fifty years, more than a hundred, more than a thousand. . . . I am looking down the long ribbon of centuries into the eyes of every woman who has ever lost a man she loved.

I reach across the table and take Ginny's hand in mine.

The Unhaunting of Bald Mountain

The great black reptilian bird darted low toward me, its swordlike beak pointing at my face, its two tented wings whirring as they bore the bird swiftly through the night sky. The reptile-bird darted closer and I saw its scaly belly-skin above me, the angles of intersecting bones outlining its wings. I smelled its acrid lust for me.

I stood unable to move as the bird came down on me, but I opened my mouth just as the whirring wings were enfolding me and — screamed. My scream woke me and I lay trembling in my single bed, the blanket moving up and down with my heavy breathing. Once again I was captive to the night terrors of Bald Mountain.

From the time I was a small child the *Night on Bald Mountain* sequence of Walt Disney's *Fantasia* had haunted me. It's full of the towering, satanic figure of winged Chernobog (the Slavonic god of evil), long-haired witches riding goats, black creatures that look both birdlike and reptilian, screeching harpies with red hair and demonic faces, the ghosts of warriors riding the skeletons of horses and cows, and buried people risen from the dead, trailing rotting shrouds and grave clothes behind them. Bald Mountain was for me the quintessence of horror: a night when fear trampled reason and good yielded to evil.

Aware of *Fantasia*'s impact, my mother had put her picture book based on the movie high up on a shelf in our house so my younger brother, Jack, and I couldn't look at it. But we knew exactly where it was.

One evening, when my grandmother of the sweet smile and smooth, snowy bun came to baby-sit, we begged her to get *Fantasia* down from its high shelf. "Please, Grandma," we begged, "read us about Bald Mountain." And then we drew on our childhood wiles: "Once you read Bald Mountain, we'll go to bed."

So Grandma got *Fantasia* down from the shelf and started reading about the haunted mountain where spirits cackled and frolicked during a witches' Sabbath, celebrating the most profane of Black Masses to a musical tone poem by the composer Modest Petrovitch Moussorgsky. I shivered, hugging my arms around myself, and drew closer to the body-warmth of my small brother and ample grandmother. The house was dark and quiet. The clock ticked as my grandmother read about fiery pits and graveyards in her measured tones. The jagged outline of Bald Mountain seemed more real than the familiar green slip-covered sofa of our living room.

As I grew older, the vivid evil visions of Bald Mountain haunted me at times of crisis. A depression in college brought dreams of many dark-winged creatures darting for my eyes and my heart. The creatures laughed at me: a sound somewhere between a cackle and a war whoop. A vindictive female superior on my first real editorial job brought more creatures from Bald Mountain to haunt me in my dreams. At these times in my life I felt besieged by evil, and I didn't know how to fight it. In my dreams I was tiny and vulnerable, and I had no defenses against the powerful nonhuman legions of Bald Mountain.

Bald Mountain receded into the depths of my consciousness after I married in 1964. Jim was physically big and very strong, blond and sunny and upbeat and perpetually busy doing things that needed to get done; I would have put Jim up against Chernobog any day. Now I had protection from the harpies and the witches that lusted after my soul. I had no more screaming nightmares about winged evil.

But on August 26, 1985, I suddenly saw them all again, those nightmare creatures of Bald Mountain. They were more vivid and stronger than I had ever imagined. That was the day I learned that Jim had been killed the night before in a commuter plane crash. Starting on the night of August 26, I had screaming dreams in which I was slammed up against a door with such force that the breath was knocked from me and my teeth rattled in my head. I gasped for the air of life as the harpies and the witches darted at me and beckoned. They leered. They seemed to want me with them. They put their long clawlike fingers out toward me. My husband was gone. He could no longer keep them from tearing me apart.

The terrors of Bald Mountain were winning and they were winning when I was most defenseless: in my sleep. But no one had ever told me the devil — Chernobog, Satan, or whatever he is called — fights fair. I was losing weight, growing more pale as the days passed. My mind was playing dirty tricks on me, sabotaging my fight to recover from the shock of tragedy and the almost physical assault of grief. My rest, like that of the Bald Mountain spirits that trailed their winding sheets behind them, was unquiet.

I sought help from Hank Harris, the young assistant pastor who had come to me when Jim died. He listened as I gave a graphic description of the night terrors of Bald Mountain. "They won't leave me alone," I said, looking down at my trembling hands.

He looked at me, leaned forward in his chair, and said, "Why don't you rescript Bald Mountain?"

I went home, thinking about what Hank Harris had said. Write a new script. I had heard of a psychological healing technique called visualization — in fact, I had a book on it somewhere. I remembered the subtitle: *Directing the Movies of Your Mind.* The point of visualization seemed to be to turn horrific images into happy, pleasant ones. But could I really "image" the hell of Bald Mountain out of my life?

That night, I lay in my bed before falling asleep and I did something I had never done before: I conjured up the evils of Bald Mountain. Like a sorcerer, I called on the winged reptile-birds, harpies, witches riding goats, Satan, and Satan's unquiet familiars to come to me. *This time,* I thought, *I've got the upper hand.*

They came at my bidding, swooping, darting, leering, screeching — the creatures of Bald Mountain. I let them play awhile and then, grimly, I started to visualize them into something else. Chernobog folded his dark wings at my bidding and became Hank Harris in his black robe and white collar. The contorted visage of Satan changed and I was looking at the assistant pastor's smiling face and compassionate dark eyes. The long-haired witches riding goats changed into young girls in jodhpurs and boots riding around a ring in the stable near my neighborhood park. Sedately they went up and down in their saddles as their groomed horses trotted around the ring.

I pinned the wings of the reptile-birds and turned them into swans, preening white visions of peace gliding around a small lake. The unquiet spirits trailing shrouds I visioned into dancers at a black-tie dinner, the ladies trailing pale summer-colored shawls, the men officer-orderly in satin bow ties and cummerbunds. The whirring and the cackling and the cacophony had become the muted tunes of a small string ensemble playing love songs. I fell asleep quietly.

I didn't manage the unhaunting of Bald Mountain overnight, and I'm still working on imaging its terrors out of my mind. But I've learned something about the personal power of evil. External objects, creatures, and events, be they as vivid as the hell of Bald Mountain, can only haunt and torment us if we give them the power to do so. If I hadn't imagined that first powerful mental script, Bald Mountain would never have been able to terrorize me.

From my earliest childhood I had invested the Bald Mountain sequence of *Fantasia* with sinister, occult powers. I had woven a spine-chilling mystique about the harpies, witches, and winged creatures of night. I had allowed them to celebrate the Black Mass freely in my dreams. I had given them a playground in my mind.

I bought a copy of the *Fantasia* picture book for myself to symbolize my new freedom from the night terrors inside it. I don't keep the book on a high shelf as my mother did. I put the closed-up evils of Bald Mountain on my bedroom bureau.

Under a Bible.

Touch of the Healer in Sestroretsk

We have come by motor coach to Sestroretsk, a town of some thirty thousand about one and a half hours northwest of St. Petersburg, Russia, to see a rehabilitation center in what was once part of the Union of Soviet Socialist Republics (U.S.S.R.). As a member of a twelve-person delegation of American journalists assembled by People to People International's Citizen Ambassador Program, I am in this facility to find out how doctors and other health professionals restore the bodies of people who have suffered broken bones in accidents, strokes, spinal cord injuries, and traumas to the brain.

The Sestroretsk Rehabilitation Center looks more like a prison than a hospital. A massive hulk of cement blocks, the building is typical of many strictly functional structures erected during the Communist era prior to the dissolution of the U.S.S.R. in 1991. While visitors to nearby St. Petersburg — once Russia's czarist capital — can partake of a bountiful cultural banquet of nearly three million exhibits of exquisite art, sculpture, archaeological finds, porcelain, and furniture collections begun in the 1700s by Catherine the Great at the Hermitage, her winter palace, there is nothing here in this bleak building to please the eye.

As in most of Russia, money is a problem here, and this facility is underfunded by the government by thirty percent; patient fees must make up the difference. The halls are long and dimly lit, the walls badly in need of two or three coats of light-colored paint and unadorned with posters, wallpaper, or artwork. The floors are covered with tile that is coming loose here and there underfoot. No vases of flowers relieve the surfaces of the sparsely spaced tables or desks, although we have seen outdoor flower vendors everywhere we've gone in Moscow and St. Petersburg.

But this is a building of surprises in a country of surprises. Escorted down yet another long, dreary hall half-lit with grayish light, we come upon something totally unexpected: a small chapel. Like one of Catherine the Great's many rare jewels, this room glows from within, alight with candles and the reflections from as many gilded icons of the virgin Mary and Jesus as could be hung on the chapel's walls. A

Russian Orthodox priest is talking to the faithful at the foot of the altar on this day, the comforting words rolling off his tongue like bouquets of verbal flowers. Anxious but patient worshipers — many of them older women with traditional flower-printed scarves on their heads — are crowded into the chapel and standing outside in clusters waiting to enter.

As hungrily as theirs, our eyes feast on the glow from the candles and icons as we look through the chapel's doorway over the backs of the women's heads, and our nostrils are teased by the rich scent of incense that hangs in the air of this small room. Our host, center director Yury M. Dokich — through our interpreter, a young doctor named Dennis— tells us that this is more than a hospital chapel for the spiritual nurture of patients. This room is, in fact, a church for the whole of Sestroretsk. Here people can get married and bring their babies to be baptized, as well as worship and receive the Eucharist on Sundays and feast days.

Reluctantly, we leave this jewellike room and return to the drab hallways to resume our tour with Dokich, to learn about the specialists who put the broken bodies of the severely injured back together. Every patient is managed by seven specialists, we learn; these may include a neurologist, cardiologist, internist, physical therapist, psychiatrist or psychologist, social worker, lawyer, and a speech pathologist. Depending on need, patients are given access to music therapy, water therapy, art therapy, individual psychotherapy, electrical stimulation, group therapy, moist heat pads, muscle-training machines, and specially prepared medicinal mudpacks.

Dokich takes care to explain through Dennis that this is a model rehabilitation center for all of Russia, and that others have been patterned on it. Light-haired and trim, he is precise, measured, and somewhat stiff in his posture and his delivery. *I am listening to a former Communist,* I think. It is not hard to imagine the Soviet hammer and sickle flying over this hospital. It is not difficult to imagine Yury Dokich carrying out orders from the state, nor is it hard to envision him receiving official visitors from the Kremlin — the citadel of Moscow and the seat of the Communist government — according to protocol, his body erect as he ushered them through these dimly lit halls. Back then, there would have been no jewellike chapel in this state hospital, for in Soviet Russia religious worship was repressed, and churches were stripped of their crosses and icons and turned into Communist office buildings.

And yet . . . Dokich now acknowledges the chapel as an important part of the healing process. He does not dismiss it with a wave of his hand, or gloss over it, or hurry us past it to show us the swimming pool — with a maze that walks patients through different levels of water — or the exercise room. He lets us linger for a while, as if somehow he understands the hunger of our eyes.

There is more. We are ushered into a room with the mental health professionals of Sestroretsk. Through Dennis's interpretation, a serious dark-haired middle-aged psychologist who reports to Dokich drops all pretense at psychological jargon. In simple words, he tells us how it is possible to help patients newly in wheelchairs who say the color black is all they can see, patients who say their lives are over. He tells us that, with the right help and support, many of these patients come to a mental place where they can say that their suffering has brought them nearer to God and, through that nearness, allowed them to see that they could reconstruct their lives in ways that make a difference to themselves and others.

The psychologist tells the story of a lovely nineteen-year-old girl who came here to Sestroretsk with a shattered spinal cord and a shattered life. It all started innocently enough. Anna and her boyfriend were at a Christmas party, laughing and joking with friends. The boyfriend took a decorative, mounted rifle off the wall, and, kiddingly, pointed it at Anna. The gun, which was supposed to be unloaded, went off, and a bullet slammed into Anna's body, hitting her spine.

Brought to Sestroretsk, Anna — who could no longer walk — said she wanted to die. Life had ended for her, she said, and nothing good could ever happen to her again. For a time, her spirit languished, and no one saw her smile. As gradually as a tulip bulb gathering strength in the winter darkness underground and poking its head above the earth in springtime, Anna came to a new sense of self and hope in this blocky Soviet-era building. She began to believe there might be a small corner of life she could catch and hold on to, Anna's corner. As her soul began to heal, her body began to follow.

Through Dennis, the psychologist tells us that Anna's dark night of the soul led her to reevaluate and change her life. First, she realized that the accident was a thorough test of the boyfriend's love, for he betrayed her and left her. She decided that he had been a "light-minded kidder" (Dennis' phrase), a jokester who too easily pulled a trigger without considering the consequences.

Second, Anna changed her outlook on life. She is more serious and contemplative now and is studying pediatrics. And third, Anna has a good yardstick to judge would-be suitors. Anna can walk now, although a little clumsily, and the boys have started to flock around again. One by one, she tells them what happened to her. Most run in the other direction. That's fine with Anna, for she is not about to settle for another trigger-happy jokester.

The psychologist is very precise about exactly what Anna gained in the process of physical and spiritual rebuilding, and Dennis says "aha, aha," several times as he listens. Dennis is similarly precise in choosing the English words to describe Anna's spiritual journey at Sestroretsk. Anna had lost her boyfriend, her ability to walk, her self-image as a person of beauty, and her hope of living a normal life. Anna had nothing left to lose. Left with nothing, she could start to gain again. This time, she could gain what really mattered, and she herself would be the judge of that.

So the Sestroretsk Rehabilitation Center, model Russian mender of broken bodies in an improbably ugly Soviet-hangover building, can help people mend broken souls as well. There may not be flowers for the eyes here, but there are flowers for the spirit. Despite their long official national policy of atheism — or perhaps in some perverse way *because* of it — the health professionals here know that mending souls takes a different kind of medicine than their seven types of specialists can provide. For that kind of medicine, these former Communists defer to the master Healer.

Peace in Our Time

I am standing inside the gates of Moscow's massive red-walled Kremlin, until the end of 1991 a forbidden place for casual travelers with an American passport. On December the twenty-fifth of that year, Union of Soviet Socialist Republics (U.S.S.R.) President Mikhail Gorbachev resigned his position as leader of the last and most feared world empire, and the Soviet hammer and sickle flying over the Kremlin — seat of the Communist government — was brought down and replaced with the white-, blue-, and red-banded flag of Russia, one of the countries subsumed by the U.S.S.R. Red stars on the Kremlin's towers are chilling reminders of the Cold War.

I have come here to Russia — part of a federation whose domain stretches from eastern Europe to the Pacific Ocean, broken only by the peaks of the Ural mountain range — for all the politically correct reasons: the chance to be part of a group of twelve American journalists who will share ideas with our Russian peers; the opportunity to steep myself in Russian culture (to see a Tchaikovsky opera in Moscow's Bolshoi Theater and visit Catherine the Great's Hermitage in St. Petersburg, one of the largest museums in the world); the chance to develop new friendships with fellow American journalists from all over the country; and the honor of being asked to be part of this delegation of People to People International's Citizen Ambassador Program.

But I have also come to make peace with a dead American girl.

Samantha Smith walked here, I think, as I look at the long yellow building that was Peter the Great's arsenal, a Soviet-era black limousine driving by, and two guards standing in a nearby doorway.

On August 25, 1985, a young girl named Samantha Smith and her father perished in a commuter plane crash near Auburn, Maine, that also killed six others. My husband Jim was one of the "others."

The newspapers were full of Samantha's death, for she was a celebrity. She was called a "peace advocate," or a "peace activist," terms that seemed too lofty for a young schoolgirl.

She had won the hearts of peoples of the world when, at the age of eleven, she wrote a letter to Soviet President Yury V. Andropov and told him how much she feared nuclear war. In the way of a schoolgirl, she wrote simply and asked a simple question: "Why do you want to conquer the whole world, or at least our country?"

Samantha became an overnight celebrity when Andropov invited her to visit the Soviet Union, all expenses paid, which she did for two weeks in 1983. She went on to appear on television talk shows, and was chosen for a part in a new TV series, *Lime Street*, starring Robert Wagner. She was returning home with her father to Manchester, Maine, from filming *Lime Street* in London at the time of her death. All of this I knew well, for it was in all the newspapers. My husband Jim was lumped with "the six others." One paper listed his name, but got his age wrong.

News flash: There she is in a still photograph with her father and a Mickey Mouse doll, one of Samantha's small hands resting on her father's large one, her other hand grasping Mickey's leg. Her long, straight brown hair is parted in the middle, she has a turned-up nose and a smile that must have lighted her way everywhere she went in Communist Russia. She is wearing a crewneck sweater, and a white collar shows at its neck. Samantha's father — strong, craggy New England face and straight brown hair like Samantha's — gazes full-face at the camera with an expression that is not quite a smile, but says, clearly, *This is my little girl.*

As a self-focused griever not in control of my seesawing feelings, I had unreasonably and unfairly resented this little girl for turning the plane crash into a hideous public drama that focused on her. "Oh," people asked again and again, "wasn't that the same crash that killed Samantha Smith?" Or, "Wasn't that the crash that killed the little girl who went to Russia?" Over and over I was jarred by comments and questions that pierced my consciousness like arrows. What kind of plane was it? Why was Jim on the same plane as Samantha? What caused the crash? The name "Samantha Smith" became a source of pain.

She and her dead father had also been the source of an unkind remark from my father-in-law: "Think of Samantha Smith's mother; she's lost two people, and you've only lost one." *Only. . . ?* Each word my father-in-law said cut like a sharpened butcher knife going through bone.

Now, standing here on Russian soil in the middle of the Kremlin twelve years after the plane crash, I thought of what I was really doing on this trip. The People to People program under whose auspices I was here in Russia was started by Dwight D. Eisenhower more than forty years ago to promote world peace. While President Eisenhower officially called the first meeting of People to People's board chairmen in 1956, I knew that the seed for the program came at least ten years earlier, just days after the end of World War II — a war in which an estimated twenty million Russians died.

In a speech recorded in Europe for ceremonies at Freedom House in New York City on August 22, 1945, Eisenhower, speaking from the atrocities and hatred he had seen as a World War II general, said: "To reduce mutual suspicions and antagonisms, it is important that *people* — and I mean *people* themselves, rather than only governmental representatives — learn to know more of each other."

Here in the Kremlin, whose very name once evoked cold fear among Americans, I walk away from my fellow People to People delegates, stand by myself, and bow my head. In the Kremlin gardens, a yellowing leaf drifts down slowly on the sigh of an autumn air current heaved by a pewter-colored sky. A wave of sadness and loss washes over me — not for myself, but for Samantha, her father, and her mother. Loss because Samantha was so young and wise, and might have given so much more. Sadness because her father's strong arms could not protect her at the end, and because her mother's life became so empty so fast.

Using the simple words an eleven-year-old schoolgirl might have used, I forgive Samantha Smith and I ask her forgiveness for the pain her name had caused me in the rawness of my grief. Finally, twelve years later, I feel a bond with this young girl that ties us together more tightly than the brutal destruction of death in a plane crash. She had come to Russia on a peace mission; so have I. Only my peace mission is twofold: It is the stated goal of People to People International — to promote world peace — and it is the personal goal of bringing peace to my heart.

The biblical "peace that passes all understanding" (see

Philippians 4:7) is not attainable here on earth. But there is another kind of peace that is within our human grasp. It's the peace that starts with the words "I forgive you; please forgive me."

Part 2

Godly Glimpses
of Bountiful Blessings

Mother Teresa's Gift of Love

If I speak in the tongues of men and of angels, but have not love, I am a noisy gong or a clanging cymbal. — 1 Corinthians 13:1

Some years ago I was invited to the Basilica of the National Shrine of the Immaculate Conception in Washington, D.C., to meet with the late Mother Teresa of Calcutta, who died in September 1997 at the age of eighty-seven. I was to be one of about ten journalists meeting with her at a press conference before her talk to an assembled throng at the shrine. The meeting was brief, but — like the lives of many others who have met her in person — my life was profoundly affected by that personal contact, because Mother Teresa gave me a special gift of love.

The frail, small nun spoke in a voice so soft and meek we had to keep our scribbling pens and shuffling notepads quiet to hear her. She spoke of wheeling a sick and dying woman from hospital to hospital in a wheelbarrow because no one would take her in, and deciding to minister to her herself (the start of her mission); of children whose bones showed through sallow skin begging for anything to eat, crumbs or crusts; of rescuing abandoned babies from the streets of Calcutta, left there like so many heaps of garbage; of washing and cleaning blood and dirt from the faces of dying beggars whose last moments on earth were attended only by maggots.

She also spoke of spiritual poverty in cities like my city, Washington, D.C., spiritual poverty that she said was far worse than physical poverty because it starves the soul. She said the most ravaging disease was not cancer or leprosy or tuberculosis, but hunger for God, hunger for love. Here in my city, Mother Teresa said she had seen the worst soul-poverty of all, here in the city of power and privilege, the city that sits in the shadow of the Capitol dome and the imposing White House on Pennsylvania Avenue, the city where the politically ambitious come from Dayton and Youngstown and Topeka and Jacksonville and Savannah and "Any Town," U.S.A., hoping to make their mark on the legislative process and senior members of Congress by working fourteen-hour days in a tiny windowless staff office in the Senate or House of Representatives. My city, where motorists are so impatient they honk their horns if they have to wait at a traffic light for more than thirty seconds, where they're too busy on the Internet or the telephone at 7:00 A.M. to say good morning to a human being face to face.

Then Mother Teresa paused in this place of worship in the city of power, and she seemed to look directly at each of us in turn as she said, "Try always to write something beautiful so that the minds of the people turn to God. . . . You can make people and you can break them. Try to make them."

I sat still, hardly conscious of the place (a quiet room in the basement of the shrine), of time passing, of what I was doing with a pen in my hand. I saw only Mother Teresa's ageless face, the wrinkles a map of her years of service to the poorest of the poor, the eyes that had looked with compassion on cast-off people whose feet were half eaten by worms.

Then Mother Teresa was passing noiselessly from the room, a small figure in a white sari with three bands of blue, her feet clad in her one pair of sandals, a small person whose humility was all she needed to equip her for the waiting crowd in the shrine. As she passed each of us, she pressed into our hands a small card with a painting of Jesus on the cross, His head hanging low in the posture of sacrifice.

Here in Washington, the power city, Mother Teresa had given us a gift of love that was also a commission: Write something beautiful for God. Don't think about your glory, about awards or praise from readers. Don't try to grab post-Watergate headlines by writing something mean-spirited. Just write something true and uplifting for God.

Coming from Mother Teresa, the gift, and the commission, seemed especially urgent. Although Mother Teresa was received and honored by the world's leaders (she was given the John F. Kennedy Award in 1972 and the Nobel Peace Prize in 1979), her work was essentially one-on-one ministry to the poor, sick, and dying. She never sought or wanted fame. Her work was physically demanding and tiring, especially as she grew older and her heart registered its physical complaints, sending her to the hospital for surgery. But all she wanted was the work.

Mother Teresa had written books, but she was not primarily an author. Mother Teresa had spoken before multitudes, but she was not primarily a lecturer. Mother Teresa was a deeply religious woman, founder of the Missionaries of Charity, who had a very special gift for reaching out and touching the heart of each person she met, whether starving child, dying beggar, king, president, writer, or congressman. Although the order she started in 1950 now has houses or hospices in about seventy countries, Mother Teresa never gave up her work with the poor and dying to become a full-time paper-shuffling administrator.

It was love that allowed Mother Teresa to keep her order's many houses of service going without becoming a slave to fund-raising or administrative duties; she never worried about where the money would come from, knowing it would come from governments, from the wealthy, from the middle class, people like you and me whose consciences tell them they should be working with the poor but who let her do it. Money came from the poor themselves (coins pushed into her hands on buses or trains or as she walked the city streets), people whose poverty is nothing like the soul-numbing poverty of Calcutta. In 1964, Pope Paul VI visited India and gave Mother Teresa his white Rolls-Royce, the popemobile. She auctioned it off and used the money to feed and clothe the poor. In 1973 she was given a large building that had been built as a chemical laboratory. She named it Prem Daan, or "gift of love," and it is now a home for the ill and demented. The money has come. It has come because what Mother Teresa did was done out of love.

Mother Teresa's special talent was that she knew how to give each person she met the gift of love that person most needed. Whether it was kind hands wiping away dirt, blood, and tears from a face belonging to a person dying in the gutter, or a word to a journalist who needed a nudge in the direction of God, Mother Teresa seemed to know exactly what to say to present her gift.

Maybe it was because her own commission so clearly came from the Christ she served.

A Very Special Wedding

The chapel where we have gathered together has a glass wall through which we can see the large crucifix in the main church, the pale carved wood portraying Christ's body illuminated for this evening wedding. The bride and groom, their attendants, and the pastor stand with the glass wall behind them and the crucifix directly above them, so the couple appear to be professing their vows before Jesus Himself.

The bride is small and very slim, dressed in a long-sleeved ankle-length ivory gown with a fabric rose at the neckline; she is carrying a bouquet of roses in many shades of pink. Vivacious to the point of effervescence, she has never looked lovelier in the years I've known her. The bridegroom is tall, erect, and trim, in a dark suit with a pink rose in his lapel. The pastor of this seaside church — whom I have never met — radiates kindness and acceptance with his expansive smiles, which take in everyone sitting in the chapel. He celebrates this sacrament of marriage with a joy so contagious it must come from his heart.

The gathering hymn is a song of thanksgiving I know well. We raise our voices, filling this chapel with praise: *We gather together to ask the Lord's blessing; He chastens and hastens his will to make known. . . . Sing praises to his name; he forgets not his own.* We also lift our voices in the responsorial psalm, wanting to make the chapel ring with our happiness for this couple standing before Christ: *We praise you, O Lord, for all your works are wonderful. We praise you, O Lord, for ever is your love.*

A teenaged boy with a deepening voice sings "The King of Love My Shepherd Is" with so much feeling — his eyes directly on the bride — that no one stirs, and I realize with a start that he is becoming a man. After he sings the final verse, *And so through all the length of days thy goodness faileth never: Good Shepherd, may I sing thy praise within thy house for ever,* the chapel is entirely still for several heartbeats.

During the homily, the pastor seems to be speaking directly to each one of us when he talks about what love is and is not, taking his cues from the passage of Paul I have so often heard read aloud at weddings (see 1 Corinthians 13:1-

9). The pastor emphasizes the patience of love, and how it bears all things, and I think of the lives of this couple standing before the crucifix and preparing to take their vows as husband and wife.

During the exchange of consent and saying of wedding vows, the groom's voice chokes with emotion. Does everyone see how the bride leans toward him and squeezes his hand? I do. The pastor's face beams as he pronounces them man and wife, and when they kiss before us and Christ I can see how very right it is that they should be together. Surely everyone else can see it, too.

As they greet well-wishers outside the chapel door, the bride's eyes mist, then fill, and a few tears run down her lovely face. As I come up to hug her, my eyes mist, too. She smiles and apologizes as I kiss her wet cheek, trying to rub the tears away between greetings. The bridegroom, seeing the tears, draws closer and puts his arm around her shoulders. She leans into his tall body, her small frame nestling under his shoulder.

A special wedding? Yes, for all blessed weddings are as special as the wedding at Cana in Galilee, which Jesus celebrated by turning water into wine. A special couple? Yes, for all couples who find God's grace in each other are special. A particularly poignant wedding? Yes, for me and for all of us in that seaside chapel tonight.

The teenaged boy chosen to sing "The King of Love" is the bride's grandson. The bride will not see sixty again, although her youthful looks belie it. The groom is well past seventy, although his trim physique refutes it. These two who have come to be united in marriage have known each other for years, doing couple things with other, beloved spouses whom those of us in this church knew. I know that the illnesses were long, the final partings with those much-loved spouses wrenching. Then there was the always-empty side of the bed, the favorite reclining chair with no one in it, the much-too-silent house. The reading glasses no one ever put on, sitting on the night table; the bathrobe hanging lifeless on the hook on the back of the bathroom door.

When love came again to the wintry place of the heart, at first a tendril so tentative it might be missed, it surprised them both. I know this because the bride told me so before this marriage. It surprised them as the first spring snowdrops surprise, their spiky green shoots with white, bell-like flowers defying an icy blanket of snow. It surprised them as the call of the mockingbird surprises, the clear voice heralding an end to darkness and the beginning of dawn.

During the toasting at the reception in a nearby inn, the bride rises. Her voice is firm. If her eyes mist as she speaks, I cannot see it in the muted light. Can she see how mine are misted? "I would like to toast two people who aren't here tonight," she says. "They brought us together in love through tragedy." As we rise and raise our glasses, we see the faces of the two who are not here in our minds, and those dearly loved faces are peaceful and smiling.

Then I realize why this is such a special marriage, why warmth beyond candle glow fills this room with its round tables covered in white linen and its centerpiece bowls of roses in many shades of pink.

This marriage has been blessed from above — in more ways than one.

The Stick on the Beach

I walked along the beach, my hands full of broken glass I intended to pitch in the next beach trash can, feeling discouraged by the new litter of glass, paper drinking cups, plastic soda and juice bottles, drinking straws, sodden plastic bags, and cigarette butts I saw on the sand everywhere I looked. *I just cleaned this beach last week,* I thought. *How could it get this dirty in one week?* No one seemed to care.

Just ahead I saw four children standing at the water's edge; a freckled, blue-eyed girl of about eleven was poking at something with a stick. As I came up to them, the girl with the stick said proudly, "I killed it." I looked down at the large, flabby form of a jellyfish borne limply on shallow waves that foamed the brown sand of the shore, retreated, and foamed the sand again.

"She put this stick through its heart," said a boy of seven or eight. Then he spoke more loudly, embroidering on the deed: "Blood spurted everywhere."

"No it didn't, stupid," said the oldest girl, who might have been thirteen. "Jellyfish don't have blood."

The fourth child, a dark-eyed, dark-haired little girl of about five in an unzipped pink jacket, watched me silently.

The loose form eddying in the waves like flotsam was a reddish winter jellyfish that lived in the waters of the Chesapeake Bay from early winter to late spring. It was a Lion's Mane, which seemed too regal a name for a jellyfish until you saw how its orangish-red center looked a little like a lion's face, and until you watched how its tentacles streamed back from its facelike center as it moved regally through the brackish water.

But now the Lion's Mane floating in and out on the tide was a tangled, disheveled blob, its tentacles splayed out around it haphazardly like an untidy woman's unbrushed hair. I turned my face away; there was something obscene about seeing this bay creature in disarray, and the obscenity was heightened by the semitransparency of its body.

"It's disgusting," said the boy.

I felt a punch inside, almost as if someone had pummeled me in the stomach.

The boy, seeing me turn away, said quickly, "I like dolphins."

"So do I," I said. "I've always wanted to swim with them."

"Me too," said the boy.

"Me too," said the two older girls.

"This jellyfish is called a Lion's Mane," I said. "I hope it was already dead when you put the stick through it." I hoped my voice didn't sound too weak and quavery to these children, but it was hard to speak when I felt so sickened by what I'd seen.

Then I turned away from the children and continued walking down the beach. The winter waves shushed against the shore, and I tried to let them coax me back into a sense of oneness with the water, the shore, and the sky. I thought of the words of Genesis (1:20, 31): *"And God said, 'Let the waters bring forth swarms of living creatures, and let birds fly above the earth across the firmament of the heavens.' . . . And God saw everything that he had made, and behold, it was very good."*

The shushing of the waves and the weaving of my thoughts were interrupted by light pattering sounds, and then I heard someone behind me breathing rapidly and shallowly. I stopped and turned and saw the youngest of the four children, the dark-eyed, dark-haired little girl wearing the unzipped pink jacket. She was panting; one tennis shoe had come untied. The little girl looked at me with piercing eyes, trying to regain her breath.

"Is it, was it . . . ?" she began. This child had said not one word when the others talked about the spearing of the jellyfish. Now she wanted to speak; her face looked stricken. I put my broken glass on the sand and bent down to her. "Is it, was it really, already, really dead?" she asked. Again, I felt a wrench in the stomach, but this time it was for a child.

"Yes," I told her. "It was really already dead. I'm certain of it." She looked at me with eyes that implored, wanting something more.

"May I tie your shoe?" She nodded, and I tied the laces of the small white tennis shoe. Kneeling on one knee I gazed at her on her level. Her eyes were as dark and compelling as a moonless night on the bay. "Are you cold? Would you like me to zip your jacket?" She shook her head, no. "Will you tell me your name?" I asked her gently.

"Victoria." It seemed too regal a name for such a little girl, until you saw that she had the eyes and hair for it.

"That's a very pretty name, Victoria."

Victoria's dark eyes remained fixed on me and her lips moved as she struggled to express something she either couldn't define or didn't have the words for — or both. "Do you guard the ocean?" she asked suddenly. I was stunned. Her choice of the word "guard" seemed far too grand a term for what I actually did on this beach — pick up other people's trash. But to a five-year-old, this part of the Chesapeake Bay must look like a broad expanse of sea, and she was very serious. What I did seemed to matter to her, and what I said would be important.

"Yes," I answered. "Yes, I do. I pick up broken glass and old plastic bottles and soggy plastic bags and throw them in the trash." It seemed so little to do, and the next day and the next there was always more trash. I'd been thinking of stopping; why bother when no one seemed to care?

"Do you feed the animals?"

"Yes, I do. I feed the ducks pieces of bread and broken crackers." There were so many hungry mallards in winter; did the food I scattered really make any difference?

"I love animals," said Victoria.

"I do, too, Victoria. And we must always, always take care of them."

Then God said, "Let us make man in our image, after our likeness; and let them have dominion over the fish of the sea, and over the birds of the air, and over the cattle, and over all the earth, and over every creeping thing that creeps upon the earth." — Genesis 1:26

Down the beach the three older children were walking along the water's edge in the opposite direction from us; they seemed to have forgotten Victoria. The blue-eyed, freckle-faced girl still held the stick and was poking it in the shallow water. The smallest of the four was still looking at me with those dark, piercing eyes as I stood up. She looked up at me and said suddenly, "I won't ever — never — ever — use — that — stick!" She enunciated each word as if she had just learned it.

Then she gave up on words and threw her pink-jacketed arms around my legs as high up as she could reach. I bent to

78

hug the warm little body. "Thank you, Victoria, for that very special hug."

Then she was running back to the other children in her tennis shoes — both sets of laces tied now — running hard to catch up with them. I heard the patter of her feet and her light, shallow breathing until a breeze off the bay snatched the sounds of her running and the waves reasserted their unbroken, rhythmical shushing on the shore.

I watched Victoria run until her unzipped jacket was a pink dot an impressionistic painter might have added to the stretch of sand merging with sky.

As I bent to pick up the broken glass I'd put on the sand when I tied Victoria's shoe, I saw a floating plastic beer six-pack holder, the kind that could strangle a duck or a migrating Canada goose or a whistling swan foraging for food. I walked to the edge of the water to pick it up, but a wave pulled it back just out of my reach. *Must get that*, I thought, and I walked closer to grab the lethal plastic holder. Before I knew what I was doing I'd waded in and my jogging shoes and the bottoms of my jeans were wet with cold bay water.

But I didn't care. Next week I would bring rubber boots and wade out past the shallow waves and get the six-pack holders and the drinking cups and the plastic bottles and anything else I saw. I would work much harder to guard the bay. And when I did, I would think of a small pink-jacketed girl with dark eyes and dark hair.

Consider the Lilies

My friends Kathy and Steve, their three-year-old daughter, Lily, and I sat around a wooden snack table overlooking an outdoor ice-skating rink. Lily, who had a toasted cheese sandwich and French fries on a plate in front of her, kept popping out of her seat to go to the window and peer through the glass at the adults and children skating around the rink as waltz music came from the loudspeaker. Up she popped, back she came.

Momentarily seated, Lily looked at me with her dark eyes from under her short cap of thick, straight dark hair — the squared-off bangs interrupted on one side by a large cowlick — and said, "Here, Peggy, you can have one too." She held a limp, ketchup-laden French fry out to me, grasping it between her tiny index finger and thumb.

"Thank you, Lily," I said, taking the elongated potato strip from the little hand and sliding it into my mouth. I chewed vigorously so she could how much I liked it. "Yum," I said. There was a spot of ketchup on Lily's dark green corduroy jumper, right below the small silver cross she wore on a thin chain around her neck. Like any typical American child, Lily loved French fries. But she was more willing to share them than most preschoolers I'd known.

Lily nibbled her toasted cheese sandwich with her even white teeth (she could have done an ad for a cavity-fighting toothpaste), took a sip of her glass of milk, and then hopped up again. "Mommy, now can I go skate?" she said, looking over at the new strap-on, two-runner child's ice skates that would be her first.

"A few more bites, Lily," said Kathy, patting the chair where Lily had just been sitting. "A few more bites and a few more sips of milk." Lily climbed back up and took another bite.

"That cheese will make you grow big and strong," said Steve, smiling at the only child who had come late into his life, surprising him with the fierceness of the protective love she drew from him.

"OK, Daddy," Lily said agreeably, biting down again and eyeing the skates with a sidelong glance. She chewed and we watched, three indulgent adults held in thrall by this precociously verbal black-haired imp. Lily shifted her eyes to us and watched us watching her from under her bangs. Like a typical American child, she nibbled the middle of her cheese sandwich and left the crusts. Ever the performer, she took another sip of milk, put the cup down with a decided bang, took one more bite of the cheese, put down the remains of the sandwich, and said, "Now, please! I'm going to skate."

"All right, Lily," said Kathy. "You did a good job on that sandwich and glass of milk."

Lily jumped off her seat, picked up one strap-on skate, and held it out to her mother. "Please, Mommy, will you put it on me?" said the child.

Kathy said, "Downstairs, Lily," and so we looked around for our coats and Lily's belongings, spread on the floor around the table like colorful props for a family TV series. We gathered up Lily's puffy red jacket with the Navy blue mittens clipped to the ends of the arms (mittens with white snowmen on them), her blue- and red-striped stocking cap, her box of crayons and tablet of drawing paper, her bag of children's books, and, of course, the double-bladed skates.

Lily was so excited that she ran ahead of us as we trailed behind this little black-haired American princess like her retinue of servants. She wanted to run down the staircase to the changing room next to the ice-skating rink, and — like a typical American child — she tried.

"Lily," said Steve, raising his gentle-firm voice slightly. "Lily, what do we do when we go downstairs?"

"Walk, don't run," Lily chirped, slowing down and clutching the railing.

"Right," said Steve.

So she walked down, fast.

Lily sat on a wooden bench — nicked and scarred from the tips of many figure skates — while Kathy strapped the double-bladed child's skates on her feet over her small red leather shoes. Lily put her legs, clad in green tights, straight out so her mother could bend over her and put the skates on.

"Now, wait for me," Kathy said, bending to put on her own white figure skates, relics from the days of her late teens when she had skated in cold Chicago winters. Skates now on their feet, they stepped out on the ice, Kathy bending down carefully to hold Lily's hand and lead her close to the solid wooden fence circling the ice-skating rink. Lily put her other hand out to touch the fence, and began inching her way around the rink, stepping more than sliding. Steve and I watched from the entrance to the ice, standing on one side of the black rubber matting the skaters walked on when they entered and exited the rink.

Around they went, very slowly, the woman bending over the child, and every once in a while Lily looked up and over at us and we waved and smiled. Once Steve clasped his hands together and shook them over his head in a victory salute. Lily did not fall, because Kathy was holding her too tightly to let her go down.

Steve and I took off our gloves and clapped loudly when Lily completed her circle around the rink and stepped off the ice with her mother onto the rubber matting. Standing there in her double-bladed skates she looked up at the faces of her audience and smiled, treating us to a glimpse of her perfectly spaced, gleaming little teeth. Then she nodded her head, acknowledging our applause. "I was OK," she pronounced, saying the word "OK" like any typical American preschooler.

Except that there was nothing typical about Lily.

Lily was abandoned at birth by her Chinese mother. She spent her first few months of life in an orphanage in a Chinese village, surviving — barely — on carefully meted-out trickles of rice gruel and nothing else. Lying in a crib squeezed between two other cribs with two other baby girls, Lily had nothing to do but look at the cracked, peeling ceiling — not even a very interesting pattern. She could cry, but no one would come; there was nothing or no one to make her chortle or gurgle, as babies like to do.

Lily was too young to know that baby girls are not wanted in China, or to hope that someone might come to adopt her and take her someplace where she could eat French fries and drink milk and launch herself out on the ice on double-bladed skates, secure because she was holding the hand of someone who loved her. She was also too young to know about the back room in that orphanage — a room where, when baby girls were taken there, they didn't come back.

But Lily wasn't too young to look straight at Kathy when my friend came to select an infant daughter: staring at Kathy's curly red hair and blue eyes and fair, freckle-prone skin. Lily had never seen a human being who looked like this, but she was not afraid. She stared directly into Kathy's blue eyes with her black ones.

"She was the only baby who made eye contact with me," Kathy had told me. And so, when the baby girls no one wanted were shown to Kathy, that look was more than enough to start setting the glue of the elusive bonding process, the intimate mother-daughter glue that would harden and bring Lily out of this stark place with no infant formula and no twirling circus mobiles and no stuffed bears with sewn-on happy smiles and no one singing lullabies or reading bedtime stories about barnyard animals and going "moo" and "cock-a-doodle-doo" in the right places.

The eye contact between Lily and Kathy was enough to keep Lily out of the back room where baby girls were taken and didn't return, the room Kathy and I had discussed only obliquely. For what is really to be said between friends about the reality of that back room?

I had given Lily a children's book about a little girl who learned to recognize the sounds of night creatures — owls, raccoons — and then was no longer afraid of the dark. Lily didn't know it, but the actions of her own kind were far more threatening than any feathered or furred night stalker. Or maybe she did know it, feeling it viscerally as a baby in the pit of her tiny, always hungry stomach. Maybe she felt that threat and felt its opposite when she saw Kathy, and that's why she made eye contact with someone who could ensure her survival.

So I knew why Kathy had picked Lily out of all the baby girls in that orphanage. I also knew why Kathy and Steve had picked for their daughter's name "Lily," which was not a typical American-girl name. Lily could have been a Jennifer or an Amy or an Allison or a Tracy or a Katherine, shortened to Katie. She could have been a Julie or a Susan, shortened to Suzie. She could have been named for a saint: Mary or Teresa or Elizabeth. Or she could have been given an Irish first name like her mother, for Kathy's full name was Kathleen. Lily could have been a Sheila or a Bridget.

But Kathy and Steve named their daughter for the lilies of the field in a scriptural passage from Matthew (6:28-29):

"Consider the lilies of the field, how they grow; they neither toil nor spin; yet I tell you, even Solomon in all his glory was not arrayed like one of these." Now that I know her, I know no other name would do for Lily.

It was time to leave the ice-skating rink and go home; Lily knew it and we knew it. This child, who would grow and bloom from the love she was shown and gave, stood looking at me, her black eyes sad for the first time that evening. Lily didn't like good-byes.

"Lily, can you thank Peggy for your skating fun today?" said Kathy (for this outing had been my treat).

"Thank you, Peggy," said Lily, holding up her little arms. I bent down to hug her, and she kissed my cheek with her delicate pink lips. "Can I come back again some other time?" she asked.

"Of course you can," I told her, not wanting to let her go. I felt her breathing against me and caught the scent of her breath — sweet, as if she were, indeed, a flower. Lily didn't squirm or try to free herself from my arms, as preschoolers often do.

"Of course you can," I said again. "You can come back here any time you want to." Reluctantly I loosened my arms and stood up. What I wanted to say, but didn't, as I looked down at Lily's now upturned face, was: Thank you, Lily, for coming into *my* life, too. Thank you, God, for making sure that Lily was delivered not into the back room of that Chinese orphanage but into the gentle, loving arms of two people, Kathy and Steve, who wanted her more than anything else in the world.

And most of all, thank you, God, for making sure that this Lily would grow up strong and fearless, nourished not only by toasted cheese sandwiches and milk and her trust in our smiles and hugs, but also by her deepening trust in You.

The Thanksgiving That Almost Wasn't

The fourteen-pound turkey sat in its juices in the aluminum pan, its brown, well-basted skin glistening. Yes, it was done. I could let it cool and then remove the meat and put it on a platter for the holiday buffet table I'd planned.

For once, I'd been organized. This year, the night before Thanksgiving dinner, the plates were already stacked — eleven of them — and the knives, forks, and spoons were laid out neatly on the white lace tablecloth. I mentally ticked off the serving dishes: potatoes, salad, stuffing, bread, and cranberry sauce — two dishes for the two kinds, whole-berry and jellied. I again counted the wine glasses and napkins — cloth ones I'd have to iron. But this was a special Thanksgiving, and paper just wouldn't do.

I'd just become engaged to Rudy, and I was looking forward to giving thanks for my new fiancé, for the health of my parents, and for my young nephew and niece. Alice, six, had asked if she could be a bridesmaid, and we would talk about dresses. My sister-in-law's parents — in their eighties — would be with us, along with my single friend, Nancy.

Yes, we had a lot to be thankful for. I'd even written out a blessing to say: *Dear Lord, let us bless Your name at all times and make us mindful that all the good things of this life, especially the food on this table and the love we feel for one another, come from You.*

As I separated the dark from the light meat and put it on the platter, I began to feel chills. *Just tired,* I thought, continuing to work. The chills did not let up. I put on a sweater, turned up the heat. The chills got worse. My teeth were chattering and now my throat was sore. My head felt hot. All of a sudden I felt so tired I could no longer stand up. *Oh, no, not the flu. Not now. Not when I've planned everything and counted on having everyone here. Not when I have so much to be thankful for.*

I put the turkey meat in the refrigerator, dragged myself up the stairs, and crawled under the quilt on my bed, fully clothed except for my shoes. But the chills wouldn't stop. I lay under the covers, feeling worse and worse.

A temperature check proved it really was the flu — 102 degrees — and I called Thanksgiving off. My mother would pick up the turkey meat. My sister-in-law would have the dinner. My friend Nancy would go without me. Rudy, a widower, would have dinner with his children. My plates, wine glasses, and serving dishes would go unused. God would go unthanked in this house.

I slept for many hours, and woke without looking at the clock. I lay in bed on Thanksgiving Day with my golf ball throat and my fever, all alone in the silent house except for my border collie, Sasha. I reached down and stroked her thick black fur, then lay back on my pillow. Sasha put her paws up on the bed and licked my hand; then she settled down beside the bed.

As I lay in my bed feverish and half dozing, I didn't feel like thanking God for the flu. What had I written for a Thanksgiving blessing? *Let us bless Your name at all times.* I certainly didn't feel much like doing that now. But I tried to remember what our prayer group leader had taught us in church about coming closer to God when we least felt like it. She had said, "You have to practice the presence of God. Pray as you can; don't pray as you can't."

Feeling self-conscious, I closed my eyes and began to pray silently, letting my mind free-float and take me wherever it wanted. My mind rebelled. I thought about taking off the white lace cloth, putting away the plates and serving dishes. I thought about the wash. About buying dog food.

I tried again. I asked God to help me pray: *Lord, I may be sick in bed but I don't have the spiritual flu.* My mind quieted, as the dailiness of thoughts left it. One by one, I visualized the faces of those dear to me. I thanked God for their being. I asked Him to be with them and to embrace them in His love.

I lost all sense of time and space as my mind free-floated in prayer. My bedroom, with its patchwork quilt and embroidered bouquet of flowers on the wall, faded from my consciousness. Snatches of what my prayer group leader had said in her soft breathy voice eased themselves in and out of my mind as delicately as feathers: "In breathing we share the air with God"; "Let the borders be permeable"; "We're continuing a journey we've all been making all our lives."

Later, I don't know how much later, the phone rang. The

callers all wanted to know how I was, and I talked to them all in turn, these loved ones I had prayed for.

"It was the strangest thing," my mother said. "We all felt . . . well, it was almost as if another person were here." My sister-in-law, she said, had miscounted and set out an extra place. "And then — all of a sudden a blessing just seemed to come to me and I said it at the table," said my mother. "I really hadn't planned it; you know we always hold hands and say the family grace."

"Do you remember the blessing you said?" I asked quietly, not really needing to.

"Dear Lord," said my mother into the telephone, "let us bless Your name at all times and make us mindful that all the good things of this life, especially the food on this table and the love we feel for one another, come from You."

"Thank you," I said to my mother.

Not My Child

The baby I held in my arms gazed up at me solemnly, from blue eyes set in a face that now bore the tiniest of frowns. It was a look of concentration, not of displeasure.

Three-month-old Nathan was unused to being held by a woman other than his mother; unused to wearing his grandfather's long white organdy-and-lace baptismal dress (under which his tiny legs flexed as if to remind us that he was a boy and would one day kick a football); and unused to being the main attraction at church (which he now was).

"Do you know what you're all doing here?" Nathan seemed to want to ask.

What we were doing was attending to his baptism, and I — as Nathan's nervous godmother — was elected to hold him throughout the ceremony. Nathan didn't know it, but holding him was a sweet yet painful duty. As a childless widow, I was all too aware that Nathan was not mine: that I would never hold him to my breast, put a Band-Aid on his skinned knee, fix him hot chocolate after school, or sew a rip in the ear of the teddy bear he took to bed to keep the stuffing from coming out all over the sheets and Nathan. I would always be "Aunt Peggy," not Mommy.

Nathan did not know it, but my joy was touched by loss when my closest friends and relatives became pregnant; when I visited infant departments in stores to buy feeding spoons and crib blankets and silver picture frames for new mothers; when I saw young mothers pushing round-faced infants in carriages, their tiny bodies covered with pink or blue blankets. Not one of these babies was mine.

Now, as I carried Nathan in my arms to be marked as Christ's own, I felt that familiar bittersweet pang of mixed joy and loss. *Marked as Christ's own.* As the phrase imprinted itself on my mind, there was a brief pause in time, and Nathan and I existed in a space of stillness. The space was warm, soundless. The filled church, my own nervousness, and my regret at not having a child of my own faded from my consciousness and I seemed to be standing alone with Nathan — whose name in Hebrew means "God has given a son" — in front of the large brass cross on the altar. Light from a stained-glass window turned the molten metal into something glowing, alive. The baby's eyes were fixed on mine, and he seemed to be trying to tell me something although he did not open his tiny mouth.

I belong to God, came floating on Nathan's warm breath, although the tiny voice could speak no words. And then the baby smiled for the first time during the ceremony. I smiled back and held the little body closer to me.

I thought about what, exactly, being Nathan's godmother meant. The church service commanded me by my prayers and witness to help this child grow into the full stature of Christ. But I was not the only one standing up for Nathan at the baptismal font before God's altar to respond to the priest's questions. In addition to his parents and me, Nathan had a second godmother and a godfather. Our voices joined in unison as we resolved to help this child grow to maturity in the community of Christ.

The service was explicit about what our resolve meant: We were to renounce Satan and all the spiritual forces of evil that rebel against God, and we were to do it on behalf of Nathan. We, not just I, spoke for Nathan when we made this renunciation. We, not just I, said that we renounced all sinful desires that drew us from the love of God. We spoke for Nathan because he could not yet declare himself Christ's own in human speech. But responsibility for Nathan's life in Christ did not rest only with us. The entire congregation — hundreds of people gathered together for worship — was asked to do all in its power to support Nathan in his life in Christ.

The priest's gentle touch brought me back to the reality of this time and this place. He was holding out his arms for the baby; I handed the small warm bundle of Nathan over. The baby made no cry as the holy water was poured on his forehead and the priest proclaimed, "Nathan, I baptize you in the name of the Father, of the Son, and of the Holy Spirit."

And then, finally, I saw what the baby had meant for me to see all along. Nathan didn't belong to anyone on earth, really — not even his mother and father. Nathan (whose name now seemed fittingly drawn from the biblical prophet) had a heavenly Father who had entrusted him to all of us — parents, godparents, priests, church congregation, schoolteachers, athletic coaches, family friends, relatives, pediatricians — so that Nathan would grow up to do His work.

Not my child? No, Nathan was God's. But I could help keep Nathan safe while he grew so he could be about his Father's business.

Gift of the Wall

The kingdom of God is as if a man should scatter seed upon the ground, and should sleep and rise night and day, and the seed should sprout and grow, he knows not how. — Mark 4:26-27

Ron the construction supervisor shook his head as he inspected the cracking, bulging brick retaining wall in my front yard. "Going to have to come down and be rebuilt," he said, pointing to the trickle of mud snaking down the side of the wall where the bricks had separated. Ron — stocky and compact, with a craggy face and curly hair — looked a little like my cousin Billy. That gave me hope that maybe I could appeal to the kindness I felt was in him.

"But," I said, overwhelmed by the thought of the expense and the mess, "isn't there anything you can do? Maybe shore it up somehow?"

Ron shook his head. "Afraid not," he said. "Nothing would work. You've got the force of tons of earth working against that wall."

But, I thought, and nearly said aloud, *what about my plants?* I had worked hard to cultivate flowers along the top of the wall, and loved the way they bloomed in response to my care. My favorite was the bleeding heart that bloomed every year in early spring, putting forth delicate new-green leafy fronds — at first very tentative — and then pink blossoms that looked like tiny dangling hearts.

I had to ask. "Ron, what about my plants? There are bulbs and plants buried all along this wall. They'll all die."

"I'm sorry," said Ron. "They'll have to go. We're going to dig out the earth and move the wall back farther so there'll be less pressure on it and it won't cave in again. I'll have to cart a lot of the dirt away, but I can throw some of it under your bushes in the backyard." I don't know what he saw in my face, but he said again, "I'm sorry."

I nearly burst into tears as I watched the men shoveling my front yard, disturbing my sleeping flowering plants as they worked. It had taken years to create the garden along the top of the wall, and I hardly had the heart or the will to replant. I had returned to this house after the death of my husband

Jim, and somehow the destruction of my garden began to seem part of the destruction that had claimed my husband. It was irrational, but the feeling was real. "Stop!" I wanted to cry to the construction workers. "Let my garden alone. Let my house alone. Leave me in peace. No more disorder. No more pain. No more loss."

To me, there was something special about the bleeding heart plant itself. Maybe it was the braveness of the tiny pink hearts dangling there in a cluster. They looked innocent — and vulnerable. One sole of a shoe could crush them, if a stomping, angry person wandered down the street to my house and wanted to be spiteful. I had once looked up the bleeding heart in a gardening book; it was called *Dicentra eximia* and was a native of the forests, where it grew as high as two feet and produced pink flowers in secret, woodsy glades all summer long. My bleeding heart plant was probably *Dicentra spectabilis*, a more cultivated cousin of the woodsy variety, native to Japan and grown for western gardens.

Because its roots were wild, my bleeding heart plant was all mixed up in my mind with nature hikes with Jim and the open, natural hillside in a small Pennsylvania cemetery where his ashes had been buried. The hillside, with its occasional stunted wild apple tree, looked like land people had once thought to cultivate, but the land had convinced them to abandon the idea and so they had left it to grow any way it wanted. It was the kind of land where a wild bleeding heart might take root under the twisted branches of a stunted wild apple tree, even though the plant was far from the forest floor. I knew I was investing the loss of my bleeding heart plant with much more emotion than I should have, but still . . .

I said nothing to Ron about any of this. Even if he did look like my cousin Billy, I couldn't have expected him to have listened to my halting explanation or to have understood. After all, the wall had to be rebuilt, and that was what he was there to do.

It was now late fall. *Oh, well, maybe I'll plant again in the spring,* I thought. *But maybe not.*

When the new wall was finished, the earth on top of it looked barren, and seemed to match my winter mood. Everywhere else there were signs of decay: shriveled plant stalks shivering in the wind and dead twigs from December gusts littering the grass. My spirits crumpled like the thin brown leaves I raked under the bushes at the edge of the yard. If it's true that one is closer to God in a garden than anywhere else on earth, then I felt farther away from Him now that my yard held little sign of His handiwork.

Then the snows came, covering the crumpled brown leaves and the plant stalks that had fallen over, dispirited by the grayness of the sky and the constricting squeeze of earth that seemed not to understand plants need cradling. The snow drifted down in filmy blankets, swirled in gusts of February winds, settled in layers that crusted at night into icy hardpack.

That spring, as I raked dead leaves out from under the bushes in the back, not yet able to face the barren wall in front, I thought I saw . . . yes, I saw a tiny green shoot coming up in the dirt and rubble the workmen had scattered in my backyard. I stopped for a moment, totally still, just looking and holding my breath. The shoot was hidden under a bush, but its life force pushed it up through the earth. I dropped down on my hands and knees to see better, not minding the muddy wetness that soaked through my slacks. I gasped as I put my hand out and touched the small green tendril, not believing what I thought I saw. But it was there — a little green shoot defiant and bursting with energy, a green shoot I recognized as a plant that would open and bear tiny dangling pink hearts.

I jumped up to get a shovel, my heart suddenly as light as the air that now caressed my face. I had to find a pot to transport this little plant from the backyard to the front yard where people could see its tiny clustered hearts. I had to find a new place for it. It was spring, and there wasn't any time to waste. I had to put my bleeding heart back on the top of the wall where it belonged.

As I dug, the loamy scent of earth reached my nostrils, and it was as heady as a musky perfume. I breathed the air in deeply and then I breathed out a prayer that seemed to form itself in my mind unbidden: *Lord, please give me the perseverance of green living things, which put out their tendrils in the most inhospitable of places and lift their blooms to the sun. If they can flourish when growth is hard, then so can I.*

That Which Remains

My uncle lay in a hospital bed clothed in a hospital gown in a determinedly cheerful suburban nursing home, breathing heavily in a deep sleep. His thin gray hair was parted on the side and combed, but his face had the pallor of a man who had spent weeks on a hospital ward recovering from his second broken hip and surgery for a serious intestinal blockage. The bottom of one foot was infected, and the sore refused to heal.

My mother gently took the hand of her one remaining sibling — two others were gone, including the gracious, artistic older sister who had done the streetscape over my fireplace mantel — and held it. "Rem?" she said, squeezing his hand lightly; his eyelids fluttered and lifted, the eyes disoriented. Then the eyes seemed to clear. He looked at my mother and said what sounded like her name, and then glanced around the room at the rest of us — his eyes focusing on my father and me as he worked on our names with sounds in his throat. Then he looked at the pastor in his clerical collar, a man he had met briefly but did not really know.

Something in the recesses of my uncle's mind — disordered as it was by the wasting of brain cells from dementia — connected with the clerical collar, for my uncle was a man who had been a churchgoer all his life. His brown eyes made contact with the pastor's blue ones, and he spoke a piece of a sentence we strained to catch and hold: "Fine, so good of you . . ."

My mother had not wanted me to come. "I want you to remember Uncle Rem the way he was," she'd said.

The way he was: This valedictorian of his high school graduating class who was first in his class at law school had been imperturbable, totally in control of the complex legal technicalities of a probate practice. He had been organized, helping to keep a household of six running smoothly, stopping by the store for a loaf of bread or a gallon of milk on the way home from work, sinking railroad ties into his sloping lawn to keep the earth from eroding. He had been resourceful, making Halloween costumes for my four cousins — including the twin girls — from sheets an hour before trick-or-treat time. He had been thoughtful, canvasing local antique stores for a cobbler's bench for my wedding present, because he knew I wanted one. He had been loving, cheering his grandsons on in soccer games and teaching them how to swim, gently holding up the slippery little bodies with their arms in air-filled water wings until they could splash toward him on their own. He had been welcoming, opening his front door on Christmas Day and drawing us inside with his wide-open arms and his wide-open heart and the wide-open smile that crinkled the skin at the outer corners of his eyes.

Now these eyes were fixed on the pastor's, who had taken the hand my mother had held. These two seemed to be communicating on a level we could sense more than understand, the pastor doing most of the talking in his measured, comforting voice and filling in when my uncle halted in mid-phrase.

How much of what we said got through to the person who was still there somewhere inside the man lying in this institutional bed? I had been told he had garbled speech from the dementia, and yet somehow there was more than a tenuous verbal link here. My brother the doctor had gone to see Uncle Rem in the hospital before he was transferred to this nursing home bed, and Jack had been as startled as the nurse to hear him say: "The problem is that I have Alzheimer's." My brother had turned to the nurse to make sure he had heard correctly. He had. My uncle's clear self-labeling was all the more remarkable because his diagnosis was unsure.

I knew what people were saying about my uncle: "Can't remember anything; waste of a brilliant mind; totally helpless; doesn't know what day it is; awful for Martha [his wife, my aunt]." Most of my uncle's friends never called anymore or came to see him, but then there was a New Testament precedent for this: Even Jesus' closest friends deserted Him. How could you blame these friends? My uncle could not talk law, football, or politics; he could not converse at all. He could not keep a lunch date, read a newspaper, or even dress himself correctly. He could not remember his friends' names or their wives' or children's names, or even if they had them. He could not remember playing golf with them or attending their birthday and anniversary parties. He could not remember writing their wills or advising them on trusts. He was not the man they knew.

Father, forgive them . . . My uncle lay on his back in the nursing home bed in the posture of submission and acceptance, palms up, and in my mind the folds of his white blanket froze for just one moment into the marble folds of cloth seen in a sculptor's *Pietà,* the mourning Mary bending over her dead son.

Who were they, those friends who did not come — or we — to say what my uncle remembered and what he didn't, whose faces he recognized and whose he didn't, what meant something to him and what didn't get through, what he understood of his condition and what he didn't? When he said my name in this nursing home room with its flower-printed wallpaper — and I could certainly understand it — the person speaking was my Uncle Rem, the man who had loved me since I crawled at his feet in diapers, the man who had counseled me like one of his own daughters when my husband Jim was killed. Some essential "Remness" was there inside the person who lay so diminished in that bed, some elusive but strong force neither disease nor the abandonment of friends could take from him. This essential core, which was at the heart of his submission to his condition, gave him dignity that transcended his surroundings and humbled us, his sometime visitors.

Now the pastor was saying, "Let's have a prayer together, shall we?" and I saw my uncle's face and upper body above the institutional blanket assume the quiet demeanor of prayer, his eyes cast downward.

Our Father, who art in heaven, hallowed be Thy name . . . As the four of us prayed out loud, I glanced sideways at my uncle's face. From deep inside him, the words of the Lord's Prayer were fluttering up like captive birds set free. I knew this because I saw his lips moving as he struggled to convert those words into the sounds he had made on his knees on Sundays for more than seventy years.

Thy kingdom come, Thy will be done, on earth as it is in heaven . . .

As we said good-bye, squeezing my uncle's hand in turn, and left his room, the clergyman's face was radiant with a quiet joy. We walked out into the lobby, past the dining room where a pianist was playing the World War II song "As Time Goes By" to residents in wheelchairs, and the pastor turned to us and said, "Did you see his lips moving? I know he was saying the words of the Lord's Prayer." We nodded yes.

For Thine is the kingdom, and the power, and the glory, for ever and ever. Amen.

Coming Home

Some years ago, identical twins with the mental retardation of Down's syndrome were born to the couple across the street from me. Given the news by my next-door neighbor, I started to tremble for Penny, who had so wanted a second child — and had glowed when told she was carrying twins — and for Al, who was jobless. And I trembled for the tiny boys, who would have a harder time growing up than their gifted brother Alex.

The twins were born prematurely and were rushed to intensive care; both had major physical abnormalities, including holes in their hearts. When Al came home from the hospital the night of the boys' birth, four of us from the neighborhood sat with him in his house and we talked — about national and local news, about the weather, about yard work and the piles of leaves that needed to be raked in our heavily wooded little cluster of homes. Al wanted to talk — about anything but Down's syndrome. There in Al and Penny's house, where Will and Jamie would in time come home with their array of medicines and syringes and lengthy instructions for their care, we tried to give Al what he needed most at that moment: acceptance. We tried to tell him by our smiles and our laughter that we loved him, and that it would be all right. What we really wanted to say was that our neighborhood would be community for the family, and that we would take Will and Jamie to our hearts just as they were.

If we had doubts, we voiced them only to ourselves. How would the other children in the neighborhood relate to the twins? Would the boys' need for special care turn our narrow dead-end street into a snarl of traffic? How would Penny and Al cope with raising the boys? How would Alex, who was used to his mother's undivided attention, be able to adjust to the presence of twins who needed so much of her? Would Al, Penny, and Alex act differently with us?

Some of us also asked more cosmic questions, questions with no answers. *God, if You're omnipotent, how could You let this happen? Why Penny and Al?* And then another tiny prodding question: *Did You choose our neighborhood for these boys?* It was a special neighborhood; everybody said so. Tolerant.

Helpful. Unusually close-knit. Not a typical suburban neighborhood, really; much more like a large extended family. Everybody said so.

✳ ✳ ✳

In 1963, a Dominican priest named Thomas Philippe invited Jean Vanier — a philosophy teacher and former naval officer — to visit Trosly-Breuil, a small village north of Paris, France. The priest wanted his friend to meet some mentally handicapped people living in a home where the priest served as chaplain. Vanier didn't know it then, but that visit would change his life.

Philosophy can be a theoretical and rather abstract discipline, but what Vanier experienced in the company of the mentally handicapped residents he met was far from abstract. At first hesitant, self-conscious, and apprehensive, Vanier experienced a kind of shock to the soul in the company of the people to whom he was introduced.

Social conventions were nonexistent. The need for love was painfully clear. In a book called *Our Journey Home* (Orbis Books, 1997), Vanier writes that each of the people he met "seemed starved of friendship and affection; each one clung to me, asking, through words or gestures: 'Do you love me? Do you want to be my friend?' And each one demanded, through his damaged and broken body: 'Why? Why am I like this? Why do my parents not want me? Why can't I be like my brothers and sisters who are married?' "

Despite passage of the Americans with Disabilities Act (signed into law by President George Bush in July 1990), Jamie and Will still face a future fraught with potential stigma and pain. It is impossible to legislate love.

Things were much worse when Jean Vanier started seeking out the mentally handicapped. Most of us have never experienced the extent of societal shunning Vanier encountered among those he visited. Drawn into this world of suffering, Vanier began to visit psychiatric hospitals, institutions, and asylums. He began to feel that he was being called to work directly with the mentally handicapped. In August 1964, beginning with two mentally handicapped men, Vanier founded the community of l'Arche (the Ark) in a small, dilapidated house he purchased in Trosly. Vanier called his community the Ark because he saw it as a place of refuge, as Noah's ark was a refuge during the great biblical flood.

Vanier's dream of l'Arche as a haven for the mentally handicapped has grown into a worldwide mission. There are nearly four hundred in the first community in Trosly: two hundred mentally handicapped people and two hundred assistants who live with them in friendship and harmony, sharing the simple tasks of daily living. In addition, there are a hundred other l'Arche communities spread across twenty-six countries in each of the five continents.

What the l'Arche communities celebrate is the human need for acceptance, no matter who we are or what earthly form God gave us. Everyone, not just Will and Jamie, needs to know that he or she is cared for by others.

A sense of belonging is as fundamental to human beings as the need for water, food, and shelter. In establishing the l'Arche community, Vanier saw mentally handicapped individuals as real people with often overlooked strengths and much to give to others out of the fullness of their humanity, not as damaged castoffs in need of condescending largesse from others. "People with mental handicaps, so limited physically and intellectually, are often more gifted than others when it comes to the things of the heart and to relationships," writes Vanier. "In a mysterious way they can lead us to the home of our hearts. . . . They live closer to what really matters."

Childless himself, Vanier had a firm concept of the secure and loving environment a child needs to grow into a secure and loving adult. In *Our Journey Home* he describes Claudia, who was seven when she was welcomed into the l'Arche community at Tegucigalpa in Honduras. Blind and autistic, she had been abandoned at a young age and placed in a psychiatric hospital. When she first came to the community, Claudia screamed at night and gnawed her clothes. With the love and respect shown her, Claudia gradually came to view herself as a person of value. "Today, nearly twenty years later, she is still blind and autistic, but she is peaceful and has an inner calm," writes Vanier. "She works in the community workshop; she is a serene and, I believe, a happy young woman."

In an increasingly secular and dehumanizing society, everyone needs community. But those who walk through life with visible handicaps need it more. In competitive industrial nations that laud power and physical and intellectual prowess, the special gifts of the mentally handicapped can remain completely hidden. But for Jean Vanier, who has spent his life living among them, the "least of these" have given him more than the strivers and competitors will ever know. "My experience is that people with handicaps have brought me home to myself, to all that is broken within me," he writes. "Through community, which is a body of people, they have helped me to discover that human beings can be 'at home' with each other. Is this not the journey that we should all be taking, but have somehow lost our way?"

✹ ✹ ✹

In our neighborhood, Will and Jamie came home to live among us as family, and somehow when we saw them the questions we had asked in our private spaces didn't seem to matter anymore. I believe we would have accepted them no matter what they looked like. As it happened, God made them irresistible. Born with translucent skin, delicate features, and downy reddish hair, Will and Jamie seemed to know instinctively how to win adults over, just as all infants do. Maybe it was the translucent skin, and maybe it was something else: Their little faces radiated light.

When we held out our arms to them and cradled them close to our hearts; when we crooned back as they gurgled and babbled in the language of babies; when they crawled haltingly toward us with smiling faces — we tried to send them a message through the universal human language of touch, sound, and smile that we were glad they had come into our lives and that they belonged here.

Just as much as anyone.

Singing for Cary

We stood in the vestibule of the small church on a blustery Easter morning, eight women in white choir vestments nervously waiting for the pastor to tell us when to start our two-by-two procession down the aisle to the altar.

I was the most nervous of all, for I was new to this group and I had not sung in a choir for nearly thirty years — not since I'd been a young girl.

Now as I touched the snap on the high collar of the choir robe I'd hurriedly put on that morning, I could feel the moisture on my palms. There were still rough spots in our Easter offertory anthem, "Hail thee, festival day!" We weren't quite on key, some voices were decidedly thin and reedy, and our tempo lagged on verse four ("Rise from the grave now, O Lord").

I peeked into the sanctuary of the little church. Seeing the familiar heads of my family heightened my tension. I longed to sing my best for them, especially since my niece, six-year-old Alice, had insisted that she sit in the front pew so she could see her Aunt Peggy.

Most of all, I wanted to sing well for someone who couldn't be there in the pews. Anne Cary Eastman — who went by her middle name — had been a missionary in the Belgian Congo until she'd died of cancer at age thirty-seven. Oh, how Cary could give life to hymns; at the last, wasted and confined to her hospital bed, she'd gone bravely into a new mission — no doubt singing hymns of praise in her head when she could no longer give them voice. Today, I wanted to celebrate the joy-filled person she had been in life.

"Start now," the pastor said, giving us the signal to start walking.

I stepped into the small sanctuary with my processional choir partner, Jean (left foot first — we both remembered), and looked ahead to the window over the altar, the high vertical window with the beveled-glass cross in it. The young spring leaves of the tree outside the window shivered and danced in the morning wind and drizzle, and the window glass was vibrant with the tree's life.

I sang, looking ahead to that dancing tree, catching some of its excitement. *This is Easter,* I thought; *I'm in a choir again.*

When we got to the altar, Jean and I bowed as we'd rehearsed, then slid into the choir stalls. I felt a growing sense of calm as I smoothed the vestment down over my knees. Maybe I did belong up here with the choir after all.

During the sermon my sense of calm and belonging grew. "On Easter day our souls are freed from the darkness of suffering and Lent," the pastor said. "We don't need to stay up there on the cross — Christ died for us so we could come off our crosses and share the joy of His resurrection. . . ."

I looked up at the moving leaves behind the cross in the beveled-glass window. Now, suddenly, a burst of sunlight filled the window and spilled through onto the faces of the congregation. The new bright green leaves, as if delighted with the warmth on their fragile veined surfaces, shook off their droplets of water in ecstatic Easter morning choreography.

Oh, yes, I thought. *I can sing this offertory now.*

As we started the first rendition of the refrain — "Hail thee, festival day! blest day that art hallowed forever" — I threw back my head and sang as I used to do as a girl, joyfully, unselfconsciously. And then, as I sang "day whereon Christ arose, breaking the kingdom of death," I became aware of a new soprano voice I hadn't heard in our group before. It seemed to be coming from somewhere just behind me. But no one in our choir had a voice like that. The voice was leading us, guiding us, helping us stay in tune, keeping up the tempo.

Who. . . ? I hadn't heard a voice like that since . . . since I'd heard Cary sing. And yet, this voice was so like hers. . . .

Now this new voice was guiding us to our final crescendo refrain: "Hail thee, festival day," and we sang as if we'd practiced for a year and we brought the very cinder blocks of that church to a final reverberating outpouring of praise.

No one moved. There was complete stillness when the reverberations died. Then the church seemed to readjust itself with creaks, coughs, and rustles as the worshipers shifted in the pews and the ushers started forward with the collection plates.

After the pastor's final blessing, all my family came to surround me, their arms reaching out, all their faces glowing. Alice wrapped her arms around my waist and I stroked her hair. "Did we do all right?" I asked, still a little out of breath. I knew my face was flushed.

"Oh, yes," they said, "oh, it was so beautiful — and we could hear your voice above all the rest."

My voice. . . ? I thanked them, humbled.

"I'll be right back," I told my family. "Just let me take off this choir robe." And I went downstairs quickly to the vestment closet, anxious to join them for Easter dinner but still wondering about that guiding voice I'd heard.

As I took off the white robe to hang it in the closet, I saw a nametag in the collar I hadn't noticed when I'd put the robe on in such a hurry that morning.

The nametag said "Cary."

Letting Jessie Go

"Rudy, come quickly!" I called to my new husband as I stood in my nightgown early one spring morning looking out the side window into our sun-streaked yard. A tiny bundle of silvery gray fur was going around and around in a lopsided circle. A large black crow with a sharp beak was moving closer and closer to the ball of fluff, and the bird seemed to be positioning its stiletto-shaped beak for a strike.

Rudy took one look, raced to pull his pants on over his pajamas, and called out, "I'm going down," as his brown-slippered feet clomped on our uncarpeted hall stairs. Then, just as it seemed the black bird would strike, I saw my husband race into view and scoop the silvery fluff of what turned out to be a small animal into his hands.

"I just made it," said a panting Rudy, cradling the little creature in the palm of his hand as I came into sight in hastily thrown-on jogging clothes. We were both breathing hard. The animal had tiny black "hands" with pink fingers that looked as if she were wearing fingerless gloves. She spread them on Rudy's skin as if to find her footing. Then she looked at us warily with bright, buttonlike black eyes, raised her pointed pink nose, and hissed once at us.

"What is she?" I asked.

"A baby opossum," he replied. "She's scared and dazed."

I hesitated, wondering if I should be touching this wild creature. How alien Rudy's smooth hands must have felt to her, so different from her mother's soft silvery fur. How alone she must have felt, so lost and separated from the other babies of her litter that had clung to their mother and nursed. I reached out and stroked her, trying to send her a message through my fingers that she could trust us, and I felt the tense little body relax. She lowered her nose; there were no more hisses.

I don't know how we knew the baby opossum was a she, but Jessie, as we named her, was quickly adopted into our neighborhood. We worried that she might be too tiny to eat anything but her mother's milk, so my no-nonsense neighbor Paula, a former biology teacher who loved all animals, called a mammal expert and friend at the Smithsonian Institution.

We needn't have worried about opossum milk; Jessie loved dried cat food, apples, hamburger meat, and insects of any kind.

Jessie spent part of the time across the street with Paula, her menagerie of animals, and her three small children, who carried Jessie around like an animated stuffed toy, and part of the time with Rudy and me. Shared custody, Paula called it. Jessie had an indoor box, and Rudy made an outdoor cage for her of pine and chicken wire so she could feel the summer breezes on her fur and smell the summer smells. Even as I cared for Jessie with Rudy and Paula, I knew we would have to let her go. How would we know when it was time? Could we do it?

In some half-realized way, losing Jessie was linked in my mind with other losses: the loss of Jim and the loss of my dog Sasha, the limpid-eyed border collie whose black head on my knee had comforted me when I cried after Jim's death. In another half-realized way, finding Jessie was linked to my new life with Rudy. In nurturing her, we were nurturing the life we were building together. Jessie had not been a part of our lives during our long struggle to pass through the seasons of grief; we saw Jessie as a freely given sign of the joy of rebirth.

Since she was nocturnal, Jessie preferred to sleep during the day and play at night, but she seemed to adapt her schedule to ours. She was always ready to be held, and never minded being awakened. She loved to be carried around cradled against my stomach in a long tee shirt, with part of the fabric over her head. With her docile, gentle manner Jessie — who never showed fear after that first wary hiss — seemed to personify simple trust. Left alone in the middle of a floor, she would quickly run for a dark place under a chair, as if feeling abandoned and needing to hide for security. But in our arms she relaxed, content to be cuddled and loved.

"She doesn't seem like a wild animal," Paula, Rudy, and I found ourselves repeating as we picked her up or offered her one of her favorite treats. I couldn't help comparing the utter dependency of this small wild animal on us to the trust we're asked to have in God. It was all too apparent that Jessie might have an insight we didn't. Too often we felt less like Jessie and more like the disciple Philip, who demanded concrete evidence: "Lord, show us the Father, and we shall be satisfied" (John 14:8). Or the ever-doubting, practical Thomas, who asked, "Lord, we do not know where you are going; how can we know the way?" (John 14:5).

Did Jessie sense that Rudy was delivering her from death when he saved her from the predatory crow? Could she feel our love in our hands and voices? How could she be so certain we would give her what was best for her? Why did she prefer being held to hiding in dark places? Didn't she ever think of escaping and being on her own?

Jessie grew fast, and in a few months she was the size of a full-grown opossum. She was sleek, with thick fur on her back, a pure white furry whiskered face, and a larger version of that pale pink pointed nose she had raised at us when we had rescued her. It was Paula who finally put into words what we'd all been dreading: letting Jessie go. She was so much a part of our lives in the neighborhood — and of Rudy's and my new life together — that none of us had wanted to face it.

But the time seemed to have come when — in one furious daytime burst of energy that was totally unlike her — Jessie raced around Paula's back porch trying to gather scraps to build a nest. Finally, after pulling together a pile of shredded paper pieces and rags in one corner of her box, Jessie fell asleep on top of it, exhausted.

"I guess we'll have to do it," I said. "It's not fair to her to keep her." Tears pricked my eyelids.

"Tomorrow," said Rudy.

"Tomorrow," agreed Paula.

We couldn't look at one another.

We chose a protected place in my backyard with bushes and large broad-leafed hosta lilies. "She'll feel safe here," I said, thinking of Jessie hidden and protected in the sheltering sanctuary of hosta leaves. "Then, when she's ready, she can strike out on her own."

I put her down gently among the foot-high green lilies, my hands trembling slightly. *I'll never hold and touch you again,* I thought, tears starting down my cheeks, and somehow these tears were for Jim and Sasha, too. We couldn't see Jessie's fur as she crawled through the hosta lilies low to the ground, but we knew where she was because the lily leaves rustled and shook slightly as she passed. She was heading for the backyard, away from the house and us. I turned away. "Well," I said, wiping my eyes, "I guess I'll go do the wash." Rudy hugged me and kissed the tears on my face. Then he started for the garage and Paula headed across the street to her house and her children.

Dreading the still lilies that would mean she was gone, I turned around to say my own last good-bye to Jessie, standing alone. But . . . the lilies weren't still. A broad leaf shivered . . . and then another and another . . . this time close to where I was standing. Hardly believing, I watched as the lily leaves bent and shook in an advancing pathway directly toward me. There was a pause of stillness. A mockingbird called from a high branch of tulip poplar. The grass seemed very green. A shaft of sunlight lightened a spot in the lily leaf patch.

Then, just there, a pale pink nose and then a white face separated the lilies and Jessie crawled out into the open grass. Her eyes, not made for seeing in daylight, were round and bright. Without pausing, she crawled toward me on her black paws with pink tips and sat down at my feet. I bent to pick her up and cradle her against me and bring her home. I breathed a prayer of thanks for this small gift of grace from the wild: Thanks, Jessie; thank you for a lesson in trust.

And Jesus said to Philip, "Have I been with you so long, and yet you do not know me, Philip?" (John 14:9).

People of Hope

David B. Larson, M.D., president of the nonprofit National Institute for Healthcare Research, is another of the breed of new scientists who are recognizing the power of hope in general, and religious belief specifically, in helping people stay well. Larson has found that religion is highly beneficial in more than eighty percent of cases reported in psychiatric research. He has found that regular church attendance, prayer, and the support systems available in parishes are major factors in helping people cope with both physical and mental health problems. Specifically, he has found that people with religious faith are far less likely to become alcoholics or commit suicide than those with no such faith. Faith in God seems to deepen when religious people face crises; instead of turning people of hope away from God, suffering seems to strengthen them, Larson has found.

Like Herbert Benson, M.D., a cardiologist who showed that meditation can lower blood pressure, James S. Gordon, M.D., is another Harvard-trained doctor. But he is not a cardiologist; he is a psychiatrist who has become convinced of the power of hope to help people heal. Gordon is the founder and director of the Center for Mind-Body Medicine in Washington, D.C. He is also a professor of psychiatry and family medicine at Georgetown University School of Medicine, and served as the first chairman of an advisory council of the National Institutes of Health's Office of Alternative Medicine.

Gordon, a renaissance man and author of *Manifesto for a New Medicine* (Addison-Wesley Publishing Company, Inc., 1996), knows the healing value of alternative medicine such as meditation, prayer, herbalism, massage, and nutritional therapies as well as the importance of traditional medicine. What he's really trying to do is put the two together. Most of all, he knows the value of hope — because he sees its presence or absence in his patients. He is intrigued by recent studies on the effects of intercessory prayer, which suggest that at least part of the healing techniques used by Jesus and His disciples might still be a vital component of health care two thousand years later.

Gordon cites studies by Randolph Byrd, M.D., a cardiologist at the University of California Medical Center. Byrd divided 393 heart disease patients in a coronary care unit — over a ten-month period — into two groups, one prayed for daily and the other not prayed for. Other than prayer, both groups got exactly the same medical care. The people who were doing the intercessory praying didn't know the patients, but were given a piece of paper on which the patient's first name and medical condition were written. The results of this study were so amazing they must have surprised even Byrd himself. The prayed-for patients had fewer cardiac arrests, fewer serious episodes of congestive heart failure (a chronic condition caused by a weakened heart), and fewer cases of pneumonia (which can be fatal to very ill people) than the unprayed-for patients. The prayed-for patients also required drugs such as antibiotics and diuretics (which draw fluid from the body) much less often, and spent less time in the coronary care unit, where the most seriously ill heart disease patients are treated.

The growing scientific acceptance that a person's degree of hope — which often manifests itself in religious belief — really does make a difference comes as no surprise to people of faith. A churchgoing friend who is a colon cancer survivor told me that the toxic chemotherapy she was taking for her colon cancer made her sicker than her cancer, so sick that she was on the point of giving up hope, until she went to the Center for Mind-Body Medicine. There her mental mind-set was treated as every bit as important to her healing as the chemotherapy her oncologist was giving her. She is not exaggerating when she credits the center with helping to save her life.

Hope — the biblical conviction that God is in charge and works for the best — is a mark of Christian believers. Christians hope because God assures us that we, through the life and resurrection of Jesus, will join an eternal kingdom where there are no tears, pain, or sorrow.

We also hope because God assures us — through the words of Jesus, through the mystical passages in Revelation, and through small or large miracles in our own lives — that His plan will one day be fulfilled on earth. Indeed, a hope that things will get better and that human beings will learn to live in harmony and grace is the foundation of our faith.

Christian hope is not an ephemeral illusion based on self-deception. Nor is it a license to live our lives passively because God will take care of everything. Rather, this kind of hope is based on the belief that God is firmly in control, but that He works through those who believe in helping Him get His work done on earth.

The ability to be hopeful does not mean that a person never feels sadness, anger, or discouragement. What it does mean is that these negative feelings don't dominate and overwhelm a person's life, leading to a pattern of negativity. Rather, the negative emotions pass, perhaps after a period of grieving or praying to God out of rage or despair.

St. Paul is a prototype of religious hope in the face of obstacles. He endured prison, shipwrecks, and physical abuse for the sake of his faith in Jesus, but he didn't view Christianity as a hopeless sentence of doom. Instead, his writings are full of exhortations to be cheerful, joyful, and grateful to God for whatever He sends.

St. Paul stresses the positive nature of Christian belief when he says, "Rejoice always," and "give thanks in all circumstances; for this is the will of God in Christ Jesus for you," and "hold fast what is good" (1 Thessalonians 5:16, 18, 21).

Although Jesus is often depicted in religious paintings as a pale, thin young man with a sad expression, that is not the image that emerges from the New Testament. As He traveled with His disciples, Jesus enjoyed fellowship with many different people at suppers and weddings. No doubt He laughed, joked, and otherwise enjoyed Himself. Although we don't know a great deal about His daily life, we do know that Jesus was a man of unprecedented magnetism who was able to draw crowds to Him and that what He said had enough influence over people to change their lives completely. Had He or His message been dour and gloomy, it is very doubtful that tax collectors, rich men, prostitutes, fishermen, and people from many other walks of life would have responded. Instead, they probably would have continued on in exactly the life patterns they had chosen for themselves.

To be people of hope takes courage, for it is easy to become despondent in a world of turmoil, starvation, hatred, and killing. But we are charged with persisting in our faith, just like the early Christians, confident in the belief that all things work for the best in those who love God.

Therefore, let us take into our hearts these words of St. Paul: "All of you are children of the light and children of the day. We are not of the night or of darkness" (1 Thessalonians 5:5, *New American Bible*).

Working for Tomorrow Today

Another writer and I were talking in the newsroom of a downtown Washington, D.C., hotel during an international convention. He cleared his throat, shifted the weight on his feet, and blurted out how sorry he was to learn of the death of my husband Rudy. He cleared his throat again, and began to tell me of his wife's painful, lingering death due to cancer. He cut the story of her treatments and her medications short, and said, "There isn't anything worse than losing your life."

I looked at my colleague as the words filtered into my consciousness and their meaning imprinted itself on my mind. Around us computer keys were clacking and phones were ringing as reporters worked to file stories on deadline. A fax machine was making little snicking noises as a sheet of paper passed through it. Daily newspapers were strewn on tables. Someone had spilled coffee on the reddish rug and the stain had spread out into an abstract artist's version of a hand-print.

I raised my eyes from the brown stain on the rug and looked at my colleague. I could have agreed with what he said. I could have said nothing and nodded my head. I could have made some noncommittal conversational response that might have been partially swallowed up in the news-noisi-ness of the room like a cough or a laugh. I chose not to. "I really don't feel that way," I said. "I like to think that Rudy and your wife have gone on to a wondrous new life that you and I can't even imagine." After I said it, there was silence between us. Then my colleague looked at me, his eyes filling with the unshed tears he had stored up for her, the tears that had not yet left the deep place in his heart where the tears started.

"Are you sure about that?" he asked in a voice so low I had to step closer to hear his words over the clacking of the computers and the snick-snicking of the fax machine and the insistent ringing of the telephones.

"Yes," I said. "I'm as sure as any of us can be without having gone there." Then I touched his arm, lightly. "You'll be with her again," I said. I think he would have thanked me, but he couldn't because of the tears he was desperately trying to hold back. Tears don't belong in a newsroom, and we both knew it.

"Well," he said finally, "I've got a story to file." And so the moment ended, and he went to find a computer and a phone and join the clacking and the ringing and think other thoughts.

I don't know if I brought comfort to my colleague. I'd like to think I did. Saying the words I said to him aloud was an affirmation of the message of Easter, a personal realization that the scriptural messages of the New Testament are more than verses on paper.

Jesus said, "Because I live, you will live also" (John 14:19). Life in Christ, our Scriptures tell us, is a life of joy, of victory over sin and death. The language of the New Testament emphasizes that this earthly life is not our final goal, that it is but a passage, a spiritual journey to another life we cannot yet comprehend. We learn that if our "earthly house . . . were dissolved," we have "a building of God, a house not made with hands, eternal in the heavens" (2 Corinthians 5:1, *King James Version*).

As Christians, we live a paradox. We look forward to a better life after this one, and yet we know there is much to do here. Looking forward to a better life does not turn us into passive observers sitting in a spiritual waiting room, but into hard workers who want to put Christ's teachings into practice in the here and now, today.

While we are in this life, we are told, we are to be "ambassadors for Christ." Because we are ambassadors, we are "new creatures," according to the Scriptures: "Old things are passed away; behold, all things are become new" (2 Corinthians 5:17, 20, *King James Version*). Being an ambassador is hard work. It entails negotiation, occasional confrontation, organization, communications skills.

The promise of Easter stirs in the ground every spring. Where there was a flat patch of brown earth that is alternately hardened by the last of winter's frosts and softened by the first of spring's rains, a slim green shoot shows the top of its head. As the sun warms this small green shoot by day, it will grow taller and stronger until it can bear the weight of a flower on its stalk. The flower will open until its sunburst petals are fully spread, and then — in just a day it seems — a brown tinge will touch the petals and they will begin to lose moisture and wither. We will not see that particular flower ever again. But, next spring, we will see another flower on another green stalk from the same plant.

And so we keep working. We do what we can to see that our young people grow up believing that spiritual values matter, that they don't have to yield to peer pressure and try mind-altering drugs like marijuana or cocaine. We support programs that distribute food to the needy in our own towns or overseas. We roll bandages for those suffering physical ailments in hospitals. When a family in our neighborhood has lost a house to fire or flood, we collect money to help them build again.

And, to strengthen our resolve to be people who believe in tomorrow but work for today, we worship together, remembering that the word "liturgy" means service. Derived from the Greek words *laos* for laity and *ergon* for work, the Greek word *leitourgia* — service — meant an action by which a group of individuals became a whole greater than the sum of its parts.

Thus in the service of Christ on this earth, we become a strong collective body whose work matters today. And that does not keep us from looking forward to tomorrow.

The Joy of Birth

It was an especially hot, steamy summer even for Washington, D.C., which is built on a swamp. My stepdaughter Leslie would remember this summer, as we all would, as the summer of waiting. It was the summer of waiting in the heat for something we wanted desperately, prayed for on our knees, worried about, thought about constantly.

Leslie was pregnant with twins, and it was a difficult pregnancy. Her first months were marred by migraine headaches so painful she had to withdraw into her darkened bedroom when the headaches struck. Then, for the final four months, she was put on bed rest and a special drug to stop the early contractions of labor that scared us nearly as much as they must have scared her. That hot summer was not a time of swimming pools and lazy afternoons in lawn chairs with lemonade (pressing the cold ice-filled glass to a cheek to chill ourselves); it was a time of stress and worry.

Would Leslie be able to carry the twins long enough to give them life? Would the babies be born so early they would need extraordinary neonatal hospital care to keep them alive? Would they be normal? The ringing of a phone was enough to make our hearts flip-flop; would this be the call with bad news?

When Peter and Henry did arrive — robust, healthy, each weighing more than seven pounds — our joy spilled out in tears of thanksgiving.

All the worry and stress evaporated in the cries of two normal babies asking for food and cuddling. As we held them, we marveled as adults have done for centuries at their perfect little toes, miniature fingernails, feathery eyelashes, and skin as delicately colored as the inside of a seashell. Like all newborns, Peter and Henry were miracles. More than the most vivid hues of a rainbow in an evanescent sky, Peter and Henry were living, breathing reminders that God still has hope for His people on earth.

Two thousand years ago a trusting young virgin named Mary gave birth to her infant son, Jesus, in a stable far from her home and family. Her mother was not there to comfort her; no midwife or doctor helped her breathe so as to ease the pains of labor.

Mary's only attendants were farm animals whose soft munching or snuffling may have calmed her fears. There were no sanitized crib sheets or newborn disposable diapers; Mary made do with folded cloth she had brought with her on the back of a donkey for the journey from Nazareth to Bethlehem.

In contrast to Mary's experience, giving birth today is a highly sophisticated science. Doctors take pictures of the developing fetus called sonograms. In the hospital at the time of delivery the baby's condition is followed closely with a device called a fetal monitor. A team of medical experts hovers nearby to whisk a newborn with breathing problems to a high-tech neonatal intensive care unit.

And yet . . . whether a baby comes into the world as Jesus did — in a dimly lit stable lined with straw — or under the bright lights of a hospital delivery room as today's baby does, our joy when we hear the first cries of the new arrival is the same. This new life is a sign of our renewed hope. The tiny, vulnerable newborn is visible proof that our covenant with God still stands: We are made in the image of His Son and every human being starts life with the chance to live according to His word.

Thus what we see in each new baby is the opportunity to do better, to *be* better — the chance to heal the hurts that mar our world. What we have not been able to do, maybe this new human soul can.

And so, when we celebrate Christ's coming at Christmas, we also celebrate the miracle of birth that brings us hope every time we hear a new baby cry. That first cry of arrival is a sign that God still claims us as His own.

Part 3

Godly Glimpses
of Everyday Faith

Celestial Neighbors

The night sky is alive with stars flung there as if by someone who couldn't bear the undecorated vastness, and added all this twinkling matter to seduce the human eye.

We look and look, turning our heads, wishing we had more than an allotment of two eyes and a neck that swiveled to better view all these night jewels set against their bed of dark ether. We look and look, but we see only a fraction of a corner of this abundant night panoply.

We personify configurations of stars, as if naming, grouping, and categorizing them by what we know can help us define and make official their elusive kinship to us. There is Ursa Major, the great bear, and Ursa Minor to his left. We see Cygnus, the swan; we marvel at Cassiopeia and Hercules and Virgo. There is Leo, the lion, near the waxing fingernail moon, and Draco and Libra.

Reach your hands up toward this vibrant night sky, way up; if you could touch these stars, you would be touching the essence of yourself. For we are star stuff, too — made of the same matter that seduces our eyes in space.

The earth we stand on, the air we breathe, and the ocean that shelters Leviathan are all made of elements that were created inside stars — stars that vanished in brilliant pyrotechnic explosions long ago. As if they wanted the immortality of offspring, these dying supernova left heavy elements that will become new stars and planets — elements that evolved into life forms so varied and complex they defy the most persistent human cataloguer. Elements that evolved into us. Elements that could only have been conceived by a Creator with power beyond our imagining. Elements that share a basic, intentional interdependence.

"The sun and the moon, the cedar and the little flower, the eagle and the sparrow: the spectacle of their countless diversities and inequalities tells us that no creature is self-sufficient. Creatures exist only in dependence on each other, to complete each other, in the service of each other" (*Catechism of the Catholic Church*, 340).

Our spinning island home, the fragile earth, is linked to the stars we can see and to distant galaxies of stars way beyond our own familiar Milky Way. We are linked by the divine star stuff of the elements to the very heart of creation, a place of such mystery it can be probed only superficially by even the most gifted poets, scientists, theologians, philosophers, and mystics. For at the heart of creation is the heart of God, and that can be known only incompletely by His creatures. *And God made the two great lights, the greater light to rule the day, and the lesser light to rule the night; he made the stars also.* — Genesis 1:16

We cannot know the heart of God, but what we do know is that creation is good, and that we are part of this goodness. *God called the dry land Earth, and the waters that were gathered together he called Seas. And God saw that it was good.* — Genesis 1:10

What kind of creator but a loving creator would have thought to make men and stars of the same stuff? It boggles the mind; then it inspires deep awe. For if we are all made of the same celestial material, then aren't we linked by divine mystery to one another as well as to the other beings of the universe? Shouldn't we cherish that godly mystery within each human being as much as we cherish the very earth under the soles of our feet, spinning vulnerably in its vast, star-strewn setting?

Think of it: My neighbor Margaret out there in the backyard squatting down to pick weeds out of her shade-plant garden so the impatiens can flourish is made of God's star stuff. So is her husband, Matt, coming out now to let their black Scottie, Cookie, onto the back deck. Celestial neighbors, celestial travelers spinning with me on our island home.

The summer has been especially hot, and the violent electric storms have dumped sheets of rain onto the impatiens bed. The weeds love the heat and rain as much as the impatiens, and they grow fast. Perspiration is running down Margaret's face and there's a smear of dirt on her cheek; she doesn't feel much like star stuff right now.

I can go over and give Margaret a hand with the weeding.

Up the street, Linda is trying to pack for a move. It's slow, intermittent, grueling work when you're trying to keep a job and raise two boys, and the half-filled boxes and crumpled newspapers have turned the living room into a chaotic minefield of miscellany. Linda, exhausted and discouraged, sits down and wonders if it will ever be done. She doesn't feel very celestial right now.

I can walk up the street and give her a hand with the packing.

Mary Jane and Bill, around the corner, are trying to help a hospitalized adult daughter whose car rammed into a tree, severely injuring her. Mary Jane and Bill are tired, anxious, and worried. Their kinship to the stars is the last thing on their minds right now. They're at the hospital most of the time, and I can't do much for them.

But I can send them a card to tell them I care and that I'm praying for their family.

On the next block, Mila, who recently lost her husband, lives in a red brick house that is now much too silent. If she once felt she could touch the stars with Sid, she does not feel that way now.

I can't take the ache from Mila's heart. But I can go and sit with her at the kitchen table over a cup of tea and listen to her talk about Sid as her tears fall into the cup.

Those deep-space photos of the stars have a cosmic seductiveness that draws the eye up and outward, emphasizing our spiritual bond with the vastness of the universe. I can go out into the night and look up and up, reaching my hands high as if to touch our celestial neighbors in space.

But there is more important work to do. For if I can reach my hands up to the stars, can't I reach them out a few inches to help my celestial neighbors here on earth?

Brian's Family Book

"Aunt Peggy, catch me!" My second cousin Brian jumped off the edge of the pool and into the water, the splash shooting splatters of droplets up around him and me. I reached my arms out to grasp the squirmy five-year-old, raising his white-blond head above the water quickly as he gasped and giggled. I hugged him to me for a moment, wanting to keep him safe, until he wriggled free — to climb up the swim ladder and do it all over again.

This shared moment is captured in Brian's child-made, very limited edition family book, which he sent me at Christmas. Brian's book, "My Family and Me," has a cover with his photograph and ten stapled oversized pages, eleven inches by twelve and a half inches, to accommodate a five-year-old's drawings. We are all here in this book, all of the people who make up Brian's extended world of family. We are all here except one person: Brian's infant sister Julie.

There is Brian on the cover, looking like a pleased author, straight blond hair parted on the side and combed back with a little water against its will (normally it likes to flop over on his forehead), blue eyes appraising the camera, lips curved in a half-smile. He is wearing a dark blue turtleneck top and a vivid Christmas sweater with a trimmed tree, a sickle moon and stars against a blue night sky, a forest floor of snow, and a fat Santa. The buttons are green Christmas trees, and they stand out against the V-necked cardigan's band of red.

There is Brian's name on the cover, and it is printed twice: once as author and a second time as illustrator. There are hearts on either side of the book's title, which arches over his photo in large printed letters.

On the first page are Brian's mother and father, Brian, and Brian's two dogs. Mother is the largest and she's in front, with a red ball tummy and arms sticking straight out as if getting ready for a hug. Mom and Dad are smiling and so is Brian. The dogs, which I know to be young retrievers, have golden ears and long whiskers, and each is standing on a few green grass blades. There is a chartreuse ball by one dog's mouth, as if he is waiting for someone to throw it. Under this picture Brian's mom has printed Brian's words: "I love my daddy and mom and my dogs. I take good care of them. And they take good care of me too!"

Julie should be in this picture, but she isn't.

All three living grandparents are here in this book, and for one, Brian has shown not only his grandmother Ann but also her red peaked-roof doll house, its door trimmed with a tiny Christmas wreath. Under this drawing it says, "Your doll house is special, and your yard is fun to run in. I love it gramma when you read to me and we catch fireflies. I love you."

I am there in a two-toned bathing suit with a red top and a black bottom, and when I look at Brian's rendering of me I remember clasping that wet, squirmy body in the pool. In the same picture are my parents — my father in a long red tie that reaches to his waist. Under this drawing it says, "Swimming with Aunt Peggy in that really big pool, walking on the golf course and eating good food is fun to do with Aunt Isabelle and Uncle Jack too."

The last page is a beach scene, and one of the four people, Aunt Zo, has a red heart on her ball of a body. The people are standing on yellow sand, and waves in two colors of blue lap at their feet. Under this drawing Brian's mom has written his words: "The shells from your beach, I keep in a good place. I like making dribble castles in the sand. Just spending time with Jody, Jason, Aunt Zo and Uncle Bob makes me very happy."

But where is baby sister Julie?

She is not in Brian's book because she died at birth.

Julie — perfectly formed and full-term, but with the umbilical cord wrapped around her neck — had not come home to the crib waiting for her in the nursery decorated with little-girl pastels. Brian had not been able to tiptoe into that nursery with its scent of baby powder and peek at her as she lay sleeping, his child's eyes wondering at her tiny fists and her soft petal-pale face, skin even paler than his.

All of his mother's carefully chosen words of preparation about the new baby — how he must be very tender with her and love her very much, for she would be tiny and fragile as a china dish — were unnecessary now. His mother had prepared him so well for this new baby that she had even succeeded in overcoming a first child's natural jealousy of an interloper. Brian had been holding out his arms in pretend

124

hugs, practicing for the times when his mom would let him hold his baby sister, fragile as the good dishes mom kept in the china cabinet.

The nursery had to be dismantled, the crib folded up and put away in the attic, the changing table removed, the baby powder and newborn diapers and tiny undershirts put in plastic bags for storage. Brian had learned, too soon, that death can come anytime, even to the very young.

How do you teach a child to live with an ache in the place where he had drawn that red heart on Aunt Zo? How do you teach a child that even the best doctors and the best nurses could not help baby Julie to breathe? How do you teach a child that life is not always swimming and catching fireflies and eating good food and throwing a chartreuse ball for his dogs? How do you teach a child what to say when other children who knew Julie was coming ask him about his baby sister?

But Brian did know what to say.

He had been prepared for this loss — as much as any young child can be. Since he was very small, his mother had read him stories about a man named Jesus, starting with the Christmas story of the baby born in a stable and laid in a manger lined with straw for a crib. Brian knew this baby had been born a long time ago, and had come to earth to be his special friend and comforter. Brian knew Jesus was the Son of God, who made the whole world and everyone in it, including all of us in his family book. Brian had learned how to pray, kneeling beside his bed and asking Jesus to bless his mom and his dad and his two dogs and all of us. Brian knew he could pray to Jesus when he was sad. He knew he could talk to Jesus just like he talked to his mom.

Every Sunday Brian went to church, and when he was older he sat beside his parents in a pew. He went to Sunday school. He drew pictures of the baby Jesus in a manger, the baby's arms outstretched like his mother's outstretched arms in the family book, as if for a hug.

Brian knew that people didn't really die — they went to a wonderful place called heaven. Brian knew that heaven was more beautiful than his grandmother's backyard, with its fireflies winking on and off like tiny flashlights, and more beautiful than the beach where he made dribble castles and gathered shells with Aunt Zo, Jody, Jason, and Uncle Bob.

Brian knew Jesus was there in heaven, and was waiting with His arms open wide to hug baby Julie when she came. Brian knew that it was natural to feel sad about baby Julie, to hurt in the place where he had drawn the heart for Aunt Zo. But he also knew that baby Julie would be safe in heaven, and that he could pray to Jesus every night, asking Him to take special care of Julie since he, Brian, couldn't.

So when other children asked him about Julie, what Brian said was, "My baby sister's in heaven with Jesus."

No, Julie is not in Brian's book, "My Family and Me." He does not have a baby sister to love and hug and play tag with, the two of them giggling and running with straight blond hair flying in the breeze as the dogs romp beside them. But Brian has something more lasting: the certainty that he is loved, not only by all of us in his family book but by the One who will always be there to comfort him when we can't be.

Saying Good-bye to Ronald

My feet seemed weighted with lead as I walked up the stairs of the large old apartment building fronting Connecticut Avenue, one of the busiest streets in Washington, D.C. This part of the avenue was lined with residential apartment buildings, one after the other, and inside there were many single people, many older widows who ventured out to go to the grocery store and to church. I worried about people preying on them and snatching their handbags in our crime-ridden city. Sometimes I gave them rides home after a church service, for few had cars. Sometimes, in a window of this apartment building, I could see a pink or red potted geranium blooming on a sill. But mostly the older widows kept their blinds down.

But I was not going to visit an older widow. I was going to see Ronald, who was in his mid-thirties and lived alone. Ronald — dark-haired and very tall, always dressed in a dark suit, white shirt, and regimental striped tie — was my friend and my professional colleague. Ronald had always looked much younger than his chronological age, and he seemed to like having a boyish appearance. In fact, Ronald's appearance had always mattered to him; that was why he combed his dark hair so carefully over to one side from its part, and why his suits fit so well. He had always looked so healthy, so fit, so ready for the moment. He had always had time to talk. And I had never seen him frown; a half-smile (of wonder? of interest? of questioning?) seemed to be always on Ronald's face.

But now Ronald was dying of AIDS. I knew it and he knew it. This knowledge hung between us with the heaviness of smoke-laden air. If I had suspected it in years past, I hadn't let the thought take shape in my mind during these last eight years when things weren't quite right with Ronald.

First there had been the news of a mysterious blood disorder. Ronald had said the doctors didn't know what it was. "But Ronald," I'd said, "can't you have more tests? You have to get a diagnosis."

He said, "They really don't know what to do for me." Then Ronald's condition had seemed to stabilize and there had been no more talk of a blood disease for years. He looked the same, he acted the same. He was always in a dark suit that must have been tailored to fit his tall shape exactly; his dark hair was always combed in place; his face always bore that half-smile that made you want to go up and talk to him and ask him what he was thinking.

It was Ronald, acting both as a friend and as a professional colleague, who had encouraged me to write about the loss of my first husband, Jim. Editor of a medical writers' magazine, Ronald had called on the phone to propose, very gently, that I write an article and then had followed up with a letter. The letter was so sensitive, somehow so unlike a business letter on that business stationery, that I couldn't have thought to refuse him. Ronald had written, "Your insights and personal experience will offer hope to those who also suffer an untimely and unexpected loss." And he had put "best personal regards" above his signature. The article had run; Ronald said he had felt he was giving a more human dimension to his medical journal. He had been very kind.

But then I had gotten the phone call. He said he wasn't doing so well.

"Is it the blood disease, Ronald?"

"Well . . . yes."

"But can't they do anything? Maybe a transfusion?"

"Oh, Peggy [a long pause; I was so frustrated I couldn't see his face]. . . . Well, I guess I can tell *you*. I have AIDS."

I drew in my breath. "Ronald . . ."

"There's not too much to say, is there?"

"Ronald, Ronald, you know there's a lot of work going on in AIDS research; Ronald, someone will come up with something. . . . There are a lot of people who have it and they're working and doing fine, and . . ." I realized I was talking in a stream of words. Whom was this helping, Ronald or me? I stopped.

"Ronald, tell me how I can help."

"Just be my friend."

"I am, Ronald. I am your friend."

Now I was going up the stairs to see Ronald, whom I had talked to on the phone recently but whom I had not seen in a while. He had been in the hospital; now he was home. I would not even think the phrase "home to die," although I knew that he had worsened dramatically in the last few months. I was bringing Ronald a carton of butter pecan ice cream, because that's what he'd said he wanted when I asked. It was so little to do.

I knocked on the door and then tried the knob; the door was unlocked and I pushed the door open into Ronald's large, light-filled apartment.

"Peggy?" It was said in a reedy voice, so quietly I hardly heard it. I tried not to gasp when I saw him coming slowly toward me. Ronald's tall body — now in shorts and a tee shirt — was thin to the point of emaciation, and his dark, thick hair had thinned patchily. His face was covered with purple splotches, which I knew to be the mark of an angry skin cancer called Kaposi's sarcoma. AIDS patients, whose disease-fighting immune systems are weakened to uselessness, are frequently afflicted with malignant Kaposi's blotches on their faces. This outward, visible indignity of AIDS made the disease so much harder to bear.

"Do I look too awful?" said Ronald in his new, reedy voice. What did my face show? I had tried to keep my manner briskly cheerful, like the demeanor of nurses on a hospital cancer ward.

"Of course not," I said, going toward him, clutching the ice-cream bag to my side with one hand and stretching out my free hand to take his. "You're still Ronald."

"Come in, sit down," he said. "Please. And thank you so much for bringing me the ice cream."

"I'll just refrigerate it," I said, heading toward a hallway that seemed to lead to Ronald's kitchen. In that clean kitchen where Ronald could no longer cook, I leaned my head on the door of the freezer compartment for a minute, hoping the coolness would steady me. I didn't want to cry; most of all, I didn't want to cry. That wouldn't help Ronald.

We sat in Ronald's living room, which was furnished with comfortable chairs, and he leaned back in one of them, a little breathless. I saw that Ronald had put some pictures of himself around the room — Ronald as he used to be. The face smiling out of the picture frames was Ronald at perhaps thirty, then perhaps thirty-three. . . . And always the hair was combed just so, the tie knotted just right at the collar of the white shirt.

Ronald seemed to shrink back into the comfortable chair, his body sagging. He shifted once or twice, trying to get comfortable, breathing more heavily with the effort, then gave it up. "Peggy, I think I'd better go and lie down."

"Of course, Ronald. May I come in with you?"

"Yes, I'd like you to."

I followed him as he walked slowly back into a large sunny bedroom — where there was a photo of Ronald on the bureau — and Ronald lay down on top of the covers, assuming the position of a tired child lying on his side. I pulled a chair up to the bed. I knew that Ronald's former coworkers had been bringing him food and checking in on him. I knew that Ronald's mother had stayed with him for a while. I knew that Ronald had had a dog he loved very much — a dog I had seen — but had had to give him away because he hadn't the strength to care for him. Now, Ronald seemed very alone in this big apartment in this anonymous building fronting the honking daily confusion of Connecticut Avenue commuters hurrying to and from work.

"Is there anything at all I can get you? Something to drink?" I saw that there was a glass of something liquid with a straw in it on Ronald's night table.

"Well," he said in that reedy voice that wasn't really like Ronald's voice, "maybe some of that butter pecan ice cream you brought me. That would be nice. . . ." It was hard for him to talk, I thought. Maybe the ice cream would soothe his throat.

I got out the box of ice cream from the freezer, found a dish in Ronald's kitchen cupboard and a spoon in a drawer, and took the dish in to him. I helped him prop himself up on some pillows and then gave him the dish. He ate very slowly, avoiding the nut pieces that he would have to chew, then handed me back the dish with half the ice cream left in it. "I can't . . ."

"I know, it's OK, Ronald. You don't have to eat it." Could he see, now, how my face had shifted from that brisk cheerfulness, how it was, probably, looking as if I were about to cry? For I was, even though I had told myself I wouldn't. I helped Ronald push his pillows aside and he stretched himself back down on the bed.

"Ronald, is there anything . . . anything else at all?"

"Can you stay and sit with me for a while?"

"Of course, I'll sit right here beside you." It was so little to do. What I wanted to do was to remove the purple splotches from his face, restore his hair, help his body put on weight; but I could not do any of these things. All I could do was sit here beside him.

"I may fall asleep," said Ronald. "You can leave when you want to. . . . Just close the door behind you. . . . And Peggy, don't worry about saying good-bye."

"All right, Ronald, I'll close the door when I leave. And I won't say good-bye." I sat, and he closed his eyes, and he slept, and I stayed while the rays of the sun grew paler and paler. In that still room I looked at Ronald's face and I looked past the purple splotches to the handsome young man who wore tailored dark suits and combed his dark hair over to one side and who had given me unbusinesslike encouragement on business stationery. I thought of a medical booklet I had seen that said, "Your doctor understands that testing positive for the AIDS virus can be a frightening event and is very willing to talk with you about your fears."

Fear. Ronald and I had never talked about fear — not the fear I felt when my husband Jim was killed, not the fear Ronald felt now as the purple splotches on his face grew larger and his body grew thinner and his legs grew weaker and he spent more time in bed, waiting. Ronald and I didn't talk about fear. *Even though I walk through the valley of the shadow of death, / I fear no evil; / for thou art with me.* — Psalm 23:4

I stood and silently recited the words of the Twenty-third Psalm in my mind for Ronald as he slept. Then I said a prayer of my own for him: *Lord, Ronald is my friend. I know when the time comes to take him to You, You will look past the purple splotches and the thinning hair to the Ronald who is inside that poor, sick body. Please take him gently, Lord, because he is a good and gentle person. Lord, watch over my friend and be with him when I leave him today.*

It was so little to do, but I felt better after I'd prayed. I felt a sense of peace in that still room that I had not felt when I'd first entered his apartment. Ronald sighed, turned on his side, and curled up again like a child. I stayed and watched him until I was sure he was sleeping as comfortably as he could. Then I got up and took the dish of melted ice cream into the kitchen, ran soapy water into it and over the spoon, rinsed them both, dried them, and left them on the drainboard. I let myself out the apartment door and pulled it closed behind me.

Ronald and I never said the word "good-bye." He died a few months later.

The Visitor from Before Time

The Chesapeake Bay creature lies on its back, large dark brown helmet-carapace pressed into the wet sand, multiple jointed legs wriggling in the air, and long, spiked tail swiveling to get a purchase on the shore so it can maneuver itself right side up.

It is not a pretty creature, this horseshoe crab, also known as the king crab; but then it wasn't made for prettiness — it was made for survival. Gingerly, I pick up an outer edge of the helmet shell and turn the crab over, gently nudging it to the water's edge, as I have done many times for many other stranded, leg-wriggling horseshoe crabs. They should not be allowed to struggle vainly upside down, for these are honored visitors from a lineage that predates our history of human time. The horseshoe crab I just flipped over is an elder, for its large carapace is barnacled. The elder moves off into the brown bay water, bound for depths known only to its kind.

Horseshoe crabs (*Limulus polyphemus*) are not crabs at all, and the human misnomer only serves to enhance the creatures' mystery. These are arthropods, and they have more in common with lobsters, shrimp, and insects than they do with the Chesapeake Bay blue crab. The distinguished elder I helped on its way is virtually unchanged from brown-helmeted forebears that visited unpeopled beaches five hundred million years ago.

If we could look through a horseshoe crab's two sets of eyes back into the time before time, we would see on all the beaches of all the early springs — on nights of the full moon — brown-helmeted visitors piled on one another like rocks, spawning in sand warmed by day by earth's star-sun. It is an ancient mating ritual that has preserved the horseshoe crab's line intact. Enough tenderly deposited eggs have survived the prying beaks of shore birds and developed into young crabs in the warmth of the spring sand to scurry out on the incoming high tide and perpetuate their kind.

What is it that the horseshoe crab knows about survival? What is hidden there behind those four eyes? This creature does not pinch, bite, or sting. It does not fight. Its tail is not a weapon; it is a tool. When it is not mating, the horseshoe crab spends much of its time burrowed in sediment on the ocean floor. It keeps its own secrets. Yet its life cycle can tell of change, growth, and renewal.

The young horseshoe crab may molt in its first year as many as a half-dozen times, shedding its shell; by the time it has a mature carapace it has shed its outdated shell perhaps two dozen times and is seven or eight years old. All of this it does without question or complaint, shedding the old to make place for the new. How does the horseshoe crab know not to remain in its outworn carapace when it becomes too tight, knowing not to cling to the familiar feel of its sheltering helmet? What tells it to squeeze itself out of this external skeleton, which splits open along the front lower edge as the horseshoe crab emerges? What tells the crab to bear the discomfort of this shedding process, trusting that it will grow itself another protective covering that will be a better fit? Some embedded wisdom must tell it, for without regret the horseshoe crab leaves the shell-shed behind to wash up on the beach for a child to find, even though doing so will leave the creature naked and vulnerable until it can grow a new helmet to protect itself.

Limulus polyphemus may keep its secrets, but its life can tell us a thing or two about soul-stretching. As we grow spiritually, the old familiar ways may no longer fit right and are ready to be shed. But like a too-tight favorite coat, we are loathe to let them go. They are hard to put aside, these growth-retarding ego encumbrances: relentless ambition, self-focused pride, inability to forgive, strength-sapping ingratitude, impotent anger, a crippling need for security. They box us in tightly, but we have grown accustomed to the box.

On my bookshelf, next to a conch shell, is a brittle pale-brown horseshoe crab shell, maybe three inches across, whole but for the telltale slit at the front lower edge. This molt-sign from a young crab is a visible reminder to shed, and it comes with the unspoken prayer the visitor left on the sand.

We can put that prayer into words: *Lord, if the horseshoe crab — ancient visitor from the time before time — has known the wisdom of shedding outgrown encumbrances for millions of years, please help us to shed the stunting old habits that no longer fit so that we may grow upward and outward and closer to You.*

What the Mirror Saw

Sandy's husband of fifteen years had left her for a younger woman in his office, and I was going to have lunch with her at her house. I had asked if I could help (wondering what I could really do), and she'd invited me over. Nervously, I thought about what I could possibly say that would soften her feelings of rejection and comfort her.

Sandy* was more than an acquaintance, but I didn't know her well. I'd always thought of her as so poised and in control, and I could hardly believe this had happened to her. Every time I saw her — taking her husband's shirts to the laundry or going to the grocery store — her naturally blond, full-bodied hair was combed into a short pageboy that looked as if it had been done in a beauty parlor. She wore classic tailored clothes — flannel slacks, houndstooth blazers, Shetland crewneck sweaters — the kind of clothes I'd seen in photos of privileged women when I'd flipped through issues of *Town and Country* magazine at a bookstore. I admired Sandy. I wished I could be more like her.

Sandy didn't work and she had no children; her husband seemed to be the center of her life, and she made him gourmet meals using ingredients like endive and capers (where do you find those in the supermarket?), and designed elegant flowered needlepoint pillows for their home. I knew this from people who'd been to dinner at her house. I'd seen how Sandy looked at Tom*; no one could doubt how deeply she loved him. It was as if she were trying to anticipate and then be everything he needed. I was a little in awe of Sandy because she seemed to be the perfect wife celebrated in articles in magazines (the kind of wife whose hair is always combed and whose table is always set with fresh flowers and candles when her husband comes home from work); I always felt inadequate and disheveled when I saw her, like a room that needed tidying.

When Sandy opened her front door, I was shocked. I hoped my face didn't show it and tried to smile to offset my surprise. Her hair was bushy and standing out wildly around her face.

---

*The names Sandy and Tom have been changed to protect their privacy.

Devoid of makeup, her face looked puffy, and there were purple smudges of fatigue under her blue eyes; her eyelids were reddened as if from hours of crying. Sandy's lower lip trembled slightly; without lipstick, her mouth looked like a pale wound in her puffy face. She was dressed in a gray sweatshirt and sweatpants, a slouchy outfit I had never seen her wear before.

"Sandy, I . . ." I couldn't think of a thing to say. Finally, I put my arms around her and hugged her. "I'm so sorry," I said.

"He traded me in," she said, the bitterness putting an edge on her words. The reference to herself being traded in like a car made me think of her husband's black sports car, the one that was no longer parked in the driveway. I felt a surge of anger at what he'd done to Sandy. How could he have been so selfish? How could he toss her love aside as he would a bag of trash? There was nothing about Sandy to be in awe of now; she was like any deeply hurting woman whose husband had left her, and her whole appearance said "rejected."

Sipping the iced tea and eating the shrimp salad Sandy had made us (and carefully arranged on lettuce leaves with tomato wedges), I saw that her hand trembled slightly as she held her fork. It was clearly an effort for her to have made this meal and to sit there and try to talk and eat. She probably felt like going upstairs, throwing herself on the bed she now slept in alone, and sobbing. "He just moved out," she said. "He took some of his suits and shirts and underwear and just moved out." What on earth could I say to Sandy that would help ease her pain?

I tried to look at Sandy as Jesus would have seen her. Jesus — who ministered to paralytics, blind people, prostitutes, lepers, and those raging wildly with demons inside them — always looked through and past outward appearances to the human soul He loved. Reading or hearing His words we feel it is the very depths of us Jesus wants to reach, no matter how unloved and ugly we feel in that hidden, inner place only He can see. Jesus said He wants to draw all of us to Him, no matter how damaged, demoralized, and rejected we are: "How often would I have gathered your children together as a hen gathers her brood under her wings" (Matthew 23:37). Because of His great love, Jesus had died for us. If He loved us that much, who were we to say we were worthless? Somehow I must make Sandy see that because of the love Jesus has for us, we can love ourselves as much as we love others.

But how could I make Sandy feel this love? As far as I knew, she and her husband were not regular churchgoers. I didn't know how to approach her or what words to choose; I was afraid of sounding preachy. I felt completely tongue-tied. But I had to say something. I cleared my throat. "Sandy," I began, looking at the smudged eyes, the puffy face, and wounded mouth and wild hair, "Sandy, I think you're a beautiful person." I paused. It was true. I did think that. I had always thought that. Then my words just seemed to tumble out of my mouth as we sat at the kitchen table over the remnants of shrimp salad and iced tea: "Sandy, I think you're wonderful. You have lovely naturally blond hair and sapphire blue eyes and a dazzling smile with perfect teeth and a terrific figure and you wear clothes like a model. But you're also beautiful on the inside. You gave Tom as much love as any man could want. I saw it; we all saw it."

Sandy put her fork down. "Do you really think I'm a beautiful person?" she said, looking at me earnestly out of those smudged eyes of pain. She asked it again, "Do you really think I'm beautiful?"

"Yes, I do, I absolutely do," I said, looking straight into her blue eyes. Didn't the Bible tell us the eyes were the lamp of the soul? All of Sandy's woundedness seemed to be in her eyes. But I thought I could see something else there, something that was not defeat. As she looked at me, she seemed to be asking with her eyes for the hope she wanted to believe I could offer her. Every word of what I had said to Sandy was true; to look at her, it just didn't seem to be true right at this moment. But I was looking through and past the untidy, dejected Sandy to the person I had glimpsed within.

"Sandy," I said, "you're a beautiful person even without Tom. You don't need him to make you feel you count. You count just as you are."

I could see tears starting to form in Sandy's blue eyes as she looked at me. Then she turned her head and looked away. "Thank you," she said in a muffled voice.

I didn't see Sandy for a while because I had to go out of

town. While I was gone, I worried about her and felt guilty about how little I'd done for her. Why couldn't I have thought of something really helpful to say? Why couldn't I have spoken with the conviction Jesus must have put into His voice to make people feel loved? Why hadn't I been able to be more articulate, as He was when He spoke in parables?

Right after I returned I saw Sandy at a party, and I nearly dropped the cheese-topped cracker I was holding. Sandy was dressed in a black skirt with a sparkly black-and-gold top that showed off her naturally blond hair to best advantage. She carried a little black box of a purse on a gold chain slung stylishly over one shoulder. Her hair was brushed into a pageboy with a wave that swept over one side of her face. Sandy's deep-set blue eyes looked even deeper with what must have been artfully applied makeup. The coral of her lipstick made her teeth look even whiter than they were. The surface of her skin looked flawless; if that look was makeup, I wanted to know what she used.

As I walked toward her from across the room, moving among other friends and murmuring and nodding to them as I passed, I wondered what had given Sandy back her sense of self-worth. The fact that she was here at this party at all was a triumph; everyone knew her husband had left her. The fact that she was here looking wonderful bespoke courage and an inner core of strength. Somehow, Sandy must have felt enough self-love to try to restore herself to the person she had believed she was before Tom left.

"Sandy," I said, when I reached her, my words coming out a little breathlessly from hurrying. "You look terrific, I'm so sorry I haven't been more help to you, I've been away, I —"

Sandy interrupted me by putting her hand on my arm and saying, "You did me a big favor."

"A favor?" I asked, puzzled.

"After you left my house that day we had lunch, I went to the mirror to see if I could see what you saw. I couldn't; all I saw when I looked at myself was one big mess. But I decided if you could see it, maybe I could do something to make myself see it."

As I let my breath out, I sent up a silent prayer of wonder and gratitude: *Lord, I know I wasn't the one speaking that day in Sandy's house; somehow, You spoke through me and reached her in that secret place deep inside where she hurt. Somehow, You made Sandy feel loved. Thank You.*

I didn't know whether Tom would ever come back, although I thought he might. But somehow that seemed to matter much less now than what Sandy had learned about herself: that there was a person in there who was worthy to be loved by Sandy.

On Sunday Time

It was hot even for Maryland, the dogwood leaves curling their edges in protest of the lack of rain, the thirsty grass browning early. Dorothy, nearing eighty and very fair-skinned, hatless and carless, asked for a ride after church so she wouldn't have to walk home in the sun.

I couldn't refuse her, but I was in a hurry and I knew giving Dorothy a ride would throw my day off schedule. In my head I calculated how much time this unexpected trip would take.

"Won't you come in for just a moment, dear, to see my apartment?" she asked in her soft, mellifluous voice — human harp tones — when we reached the anonymous low-rise of gray cement block, one of several identical low-rises in the complex. Inwardly I sighed, but I said yes, not wanting to hurt her feelings. I was thinking about buying eggs and milk and a Sunday newspaper, about answering letters, about the living room rug I had to vacuum and the phone calls I hadn't yet had a chance to return, about . . .

Like others in our neighborhood parish, I had taken older single people home from church before, lonely people whose need for company pressed like a hand on the arm. They had sat and talked about adult children who didn't visit — at first hesitantly, then angrily ("Not even on my birthday!") — about doctor and hospital visits and pills, about difficulty getting to the grocery store in the snow or heat. I knew what they needed more than anything was ears to listen, and I tried to provide mine when I could. After all, I was single. I knew what it was like to be lonely. I needed ears to listen, too. After thirty minutes or so, looking at my watch sideways, I usually politely pulled away, because I had work or errands to do. I wished I could do more for the people I drove home. I wished I could spend more time with them.

When Dorothy opened the door to her apartment, I almost gasped. All thoughts of what I had intended to do on this Sunday left my mind. The apartment was very clean, light-filled and still, done all in shades of pink and white, with silk embroidered pillows — pastel pink flowers worked in tiny stitches — plumped on the chintz love seat and matching stuffed chair with ottoman, a doll collection in a tall case with glass doors on one wall, and oil paintings of young girls and women in ankle-brushing sashed gowns, dogs and cats and fish covering the other white walls. "I did these, dear," she said, sweeping her arm to take in the paintings and the hand-stitched pillows. I found myself wanting to pause before each painting and pick up the pillows to look at their stitching more closely.

"Dorothy, they're lovely," I said, really meaning it. I felt I was being granted privileged glimpses of a Dorothy I had never known existed.

"Sit for just a minute, can't you, dear?" she said in her harp tones, and so I sank down on the pink-and-white ottoman, busyness shelved like the art titles I saw on Dorothy's bookshelf.

"This is my haven," she said. "I find peace here, dear."

As I sat across from Dorothy, who had settled on the love seat, and listened to her voice, her self-created peace began to settle on us like a hush. She was dressed in thin white batiste trimmed in white lace at the neck, in a dress she said she had sewn herself. Her white hair with blond streaks was swept back from a face with unblemished skin that looked several decades younger than what Dorothy's birth date might have revealed. Her skin was almost as opalescent as the seashell displayed on a small white side table. I had no desire to move.

"You know," she said, "I've had a hard life, dear. I've had leukemia."

Cancer! Dorothy's skin, hair, and eyes radiated the harmony of an internal physical balance. How had she. . . ?

Dorothy stopped. "But I'm not going to bore you with that, dear."

"Dorothy, you're not boring me," I said, drawn by an indefinable glow I had never really stopped to notice in Dorothy before. Tell me your secret, I wanted to say, but didn't.

Dorothy settled back in her chair, her face almost ethereal in repose. From a small brass picture frame on top of Dorothy's television, three blond children (grandchildren?) peered out at us. She had spoken of a daughter, but I really knew nothing about her family. I wished Dorothy would tell me about her life. How had she learned to sew so exquisitely? Where had she learned to paint in such detail?

"I think God compensates us for our hard times, dear, I really do," said Dorothy. "I think He's given me this time to myself to paint and sew . . . and to feel love. I do, you know." Looking at her face and eyes, I had no doubt of it. Thinking about seeing her praying in church every Sunday, I was sure of it. Now, seeing her in this apartment she had turned into an inviting refuge, I could see her love reflected in every object she had gathered about her.

"Now that I'm older, I can understand people better. I can understand why they do what they do. If you can understand, you can love."

"And forgive?" I asked.

"Yes, and forgive," said Dorothy. How much had she had to forgive in her decades of life? There was so much I didn't know about her and now wanted to know. All I really knew was that Dorothy had survived a life-threatening illness and achieved a peace few people had. There seemed to be no clock in Dorothy's apartment, and it was just as well, for clock time no longer seemed part of this Sunday.

"Dorothy, what about this morning, what Father Jim said about the love of human beings sometimes changing and letting us down but God's love being steadfast? Do you think the people closest to us let us down?" Somehow, it seemed very important to hear her answer.

"Oh," Dorothy said, smiling slightly and leaning forward and brushing my arm with her fingers as lightly as a puff of air, "they let you down, all right. But you can love them anyway. That's the point, isn't it?"

Through the glass doors leading to Dorothy's small patio I could see bushy geraniums lifting their pink petal clusters to the sunlight, their thick dark green leaves flourishing despite the heat, the plants clearly benefiting from Dorothy's regular watering and the prompt picking of brown leaves and spent petal clusters.

"Yes," I said, as I reluctantly rose from the pink-and-white ottoman to leave Dorothy's refuge and resume clock time.

Yes, Dorothy, that is the point, and thank you for being one of God's gentle reminders.

Lesson of the Cookie Dough

Advent is supposed to be a time of joyful preparation, but on the December night I decided to make Christmas cookies at eleven o'clock with my husband Rudy it seemed more like a time of chaos. *How did I let it get so late?* I thought as I plopped sugar, flour, milk, eggs, and margarine into the white china bowl of our old food mixer and turned it on "low."

As the mixer bowl went around and around, the dough formed into little blobs that refused to adhere and stick together. Rudy, who always followed directions, looked at me and then at the recipe I was supposed to be following. "Honey, did you read this?" he said in a tone I knew meant I hadn't done it the way he would have. He held the worn cookbook — kept together by masking tape on its binding — under my nose. "You were supposed to add the flour to the butter in three parts, adding a third of the milk each time and beating after each addition."

"I didn't have time," I said, spilling some flour on the floor as I bumped against the flour package while bending over to rummage for the cookie sheets in the bottom cabinet.

"It's not working," he said in that authoritative tone left over from his days as an officer in the Marines. "You'll have to throw it all away and start over."

"No!" I cried, positioning myself in front of the food mixer. "That's a waste!" On the word "waste" there was a loud crash, as the bread pans and molds I had dislodged while trying to find the cookie sheets spilled out onto the floor. What had happened to the loving togetherness and joys of Christmas baking you read about in women's magazines?

"I'm going to take it out and knead it," I said, picking up the dough globules. At first the dough stuck to my hands in little pieces, but as I worked it in my fingers it began to stick to itself and become more pliant. "Please," I said to my husband, "you have stronger hands than I do. Please work with it." He took the blob in his hands doubtfully, but began to squeeze and pummel it.

"What do you know?" he said. "It's getting more like dough. Maybe it will work after all. Let's put it in the refrigerator now like the cookbook says."

Ten minutes later I took the dough from the refrigerator and marveled as I rolled it out. All the little pebbles of flour and sugar had taken on the smoothness and consistency real cookie dough should have. As we cut out the dough together in star, moon, and tree shapes, I was glad I hadn't thrown out the conglomeration in the food mixer. It looked like we could turn it into edible cookies after all.

But, I thought, *next time I'll follow directions so it won't be so hit-and-miss.*

I was even more glad we'd kept on kneading when my husband tasted the edges of the very first star shape from the first batch, done in exactly the nine minutes the cookbook specified. It was exactly nine minutes because my husband set the orange plastic egg timer. He smiled as he bit into the golden-brown star and chewed. "It's terrific!" he said. "I've just got to stop being so rigid. I thought we should throw it out and you made it work."

I hugged him, so tired by now I could hardly stand up, because it was after midnight. "No," I said. "*We* made it work."

The Man who molded fishermen into disciples and sinners into saints can surely help us to work together, using our differences so we can mold the pieces of our lives into a seamless whole that makes sense even if it sometimes looks hopeless to us. In my heart I knew I could stand a little more of Rudy's organization and penchant for directions. What exempts the creative spirit from the discipline that gives shape to content? And maybe in his heart Rudy knew that he needed to bend a little around the edges, to put the book aside sometimes and try a new method of living.

Right then, in that messy kitchen that I was too tired to clean up, I asked to be molded.

Black Elk and the Cross of Christ

Was he an Indian medicine man, a devout Christian teacher, or both? That is the question raised by the historical mystery story of Black Elk (1863-1950), a holy man of the Oglala Lakota Sioux. The mystery challenges us to rethink our concept of spirituality and the human tendency to put people in neat religious boxes, just as we box them by profession, social status, and race. The story of Black Elk also asks us to consider whether we are not all really praying to the same God, no matter what we call Him.

Back when American Indians were called Indians, not Native Americans, Black Elk was a revered mystical leader of his people who was known for his visionary and healing powers. The Indian chief had experienced what historians call a "power vision" at the age of nine.

This was a vision of talking horses and six wise grandfathers — representing the powers of the world — and a flowering tree for a flourishing people, and a holy pipe and a sacred herb for wisdom. It was also a vision of strength that was being conferred on Black Elk, control of the "center of the nation's hoop" so that he might help his people live and flourish. Although the vision made clear Black Elk's responsibility and empowerment to help his people (he was the sixth grandfather) and ended in triumph, it also had a fleeting image of woe: The nation's hoop was broken, the Lakota people were starving, their ponies were skin and bones, and the bison — the gift of the great spirit — were gone.

By his sixteenth year Black Elk had come to fear the men who gave him the vision, the wise grandfathers, according to William Portier, Ph.D., chairman of the Department of Theology at Mt. St. Mary's College in Emmitsburg, Maryland; Portier is one of the historians who have looked into the mystery of Black Elk's spirituality. Nevertheless, at eighteen Black Elk found the sacred herb of the vision and at nineteen he performed his first healing.

Then everything began to change.

In 1888 Jesuit missionaries came to Pine Ridge, South Dakota, home of Black Elk's people, to bring the message of Christ. On December 29, 1890, Black Elk saw the massacre of his people at Wounded Knee. For years after this he lived among the barren hills of Pine Ridge, growing old. He married twice (his first wife died) and had seven children, of whom the best known were Ben Black Elk and Lucy Black Elk.

In his old age Black Elk was said to have uttered a well-known speech, the death-of-the-dream speech, which was subsequently printed in a book by poet John G. Neihardt, who interviewed Black Elk as an old man. This speech became known as an epitaph for the Lakota: "I did not know then how much was ended. When I look back now from this high hill of my old age, I can still see the butchered women and children lying heaped and scattered all along the crooked gulch as plain as when I saw them with eyes still young. And I can see that something else died there in the bloody mud, and was buried in the blizzard. A people's dream died there. It was a beautiful dream. And I, to whom so great a vision was given in my youth — you see now a pitiful old man who has done nothing, for the nation's hoop is broken and scattered. There is no center any longer, and the sacred tree is dead."

A plaintive cry from a vanishing Native American oppressed by the white man — except that it's fiction.

The stenographic transcript of Neihardt's interviews with Black Elk (published in 1984) make it clear that the Indian never uttered it, and the fictitious death-of-the-dream speech leaves out the nearly thirty years Black Elk spent as a leader of the Catholic community at Pine Ridge and as its chief native catechist.

Neihardt published *Black Elk Speaks, Being the Life Story of a Holy Man of the Oglala Sioux*, in 1932. Neihardt had gone to Pine Ridge Reservation to seek out an old medicine man for inspiration in writing an epic poem, "Cycle of the West." Neihardt's book purports to be the words of Black Elk spoken directly to Neihardt. Perhaps because it came at the time of the depression years, the book was not a success. But then the book was rediscovered by the 1960s flower-power romantics and the budding environmentalists of the early 1970s. Black Elk became a cult figure whose popularity turned the book into a best seller (more than one million copies sold) and, long after his death in 1950, turned him into a cultural icon of late twentieth-century American spirituality.

In historian Portier's words, "To the young activists of the American Indian Movement his sacred vision offered a sense of what is 'truly Indian,' and an inspiration for their political struggle." Joseph Campbell, noted authority on myths, even explained Black Elk's sacred vision to Bill Moyers on national television.

But what about Black Elk's nearly three decades as a Catholic catechist? In 1980, Rev. Paul B. Steinmetz, a Jesuit priest, published *Pipe, Bible, and Peyote Among the Oglala Lakota*. With this book, which portrayed Black Elk as a devout Christian, Steinmetz stole away Black Elk as a romantic cultural icon of the vanishing and oppressed Native American. Then in 1984, Raymond Demallie, an Indiana University anthropologist, continued the theft of the cultural icon with his book *The Sixth Grandfather*. Demallie edited Neihardt's field notes for his book, coming up with different conclusions from the poet's, and the gulf began to widen between Neihardt's literary portrait and the Black Elk of history. More books on the actual — not romanticized — Black Elk followed.

In 1993, another Jesuit, Rev. Michael Steltenkamp, a young anthropologist who had taught at Pine Ridge during the 1970s, published *Black Elk, Holy Man of the Oglala*. Based on extensive interviews, especially with Black Elk's married daughter Lucy Looks Twice, Father Steltenkamp presented Black Elk as the Christian leader he was for nearly three decades. Lucy told the Jesuit priest that the greater part of her father's life was spent as a meek and gentle Catholic who brought the message of Christ the Messiah to his people in their own language. Lucy said the flowering tree in her father's vision was the tree of life of all peoples.

So who was Black Elk? In Portier's view, "Black Elk's life is a case study in what Pope John Paul II might call inculturation." That is, the Indian holy man retained his native identity while embracing the message of Christ. "Black Elk refused to set Catholicism against Lakota beliefs," said Portier. "He helped his people to adapt and led them into new avenues of religious experience. . . ." Black Elk's life thus had a religious integrity that could not be compromised by having the trappings of one creed set against those of another. In his research, Portier found no evidence for the popular notion that the Jesuit missionaries tried to destroy Lakota beliefs:

"It's simply not true that the Jesuits regarded traditional Lakota practices as a set of demonic rites to be stamped out."

As in any good detective story, nagging questions remain in the story of Black Elk and the cross of Christ. How could the poet Neihardt, who found Black Elk as an old man, have ignored the Indian's three decades as a Catholic catechist? Neihardt was a critic of traditional religion; it is possible that the multidimensional Black Elk withheld this information, knowing that Christianity would have been incompatible with Neihardt's view of Black Elk as the vanishing Native American.

There is also the possibility — raised by literary critic Julian Rice — that Black Elk feigned Catholicism as convenient and politically correct. Or, as philosopher Clyde Holler has suggested, Black Elk may have been a chameleonlike dualist: a Lakota traditionalist with Neihardt and a Catholic with Lucy.

Portier believes the correct interpretation of the historical Black Elk is that his spirituality was both truly Lakota and truly Catholic. Perhaps Black Elk, gifted with more spiritual vision than even his historians knew, was able to embrace a religious philosophy that could not be typecast or neatly boxed. Perhaps he saw an essential oneness of abundant goodness in the great spirit and the Christian Father.

Perhaps Black Elk, who died at the age of eighty-seven holding both a Lakota sacred smoking pipe and a rosary, saw in Jesus a messiah whose message of love transcends skin color, culture, and tongue to reach the hearts of all peoples who come from the flowering tree.

Divine Silence

I have a close friend who begins every morning in total silence but for the chirps of birds greeting the new morning that reach her through her bedroom windows. She does not turn on the coffeemaker. She does not turn on the radio. She does not go to the front door to get the newspaper. She lies on her back in bed in silence and begins her day by thanking God for ten blessings in her life, ticking them off on each of her fingers. Her first item is always thanksgiving for the silence of the new morning, because it gives her another chance to draw closer to God.

When she has finished her silent time of thanksgiving, she gets up and lets the day start intruding on her consciousness, as it will do with rudeness and noise.

Caught up in the frenzy of a mechanized world that thrives on instant communication, most of us spend much of our time trying to respond to the multiple demands of our secular world. In such a world, in such an era, it is increasingly difficult to find a space of silence to be alone with God.

The easy thing to do would be to let the demands of the world overpower our inner need to come closer to God in silence. After all, there is always an important need that must be filled: mail to read, phone calls to be made, cookies to bake, a meeting to attend, a bill to pay, an errand to run at the store, a TV program to watch. And, in filling our roles as Christ's hands on earth, there are many good works that need to be done — right now.

Yet Christ Himself sometimes drew apart for times of quiet and contemplation with God the Father. He recognized that, to gain spiritual strength for His mission of redemption on earth, He needed to take time away from preaching and healing for meditation and prayer. We also need time alone to deepen our spiritual awareness and share our desires and love with God in silent prayer away from others.

In the fifteenth-century Christian classic *The Imitation of Christ*, the mystic Thomas à Kempis wrote: "Choose therefore a secret place, love to be alone, keep thee from hearing of vain tales. . . ."

In our day, the late Dutch priest and author Henri J. M.

Nouwen warned that without a certain amount of solitude we are victimized by the demands of society and by our frantic efforts to keep our "false selves" before the public. The false self is the public one we present to the world, not the weak, vulnerable, needy self God seeks.

Many people commune with God not only in church, but on silent walks in the loveliness of His natural world. Others make time to be alone with God in the early morning, before the day rushes in with its "must do" list. Lying quietly in bed like my friend, we can begin our day with thanksgiving for all our blessings, then add our petitions. We can silently read God's word in the holy Scriptures, the spiritual food that nourishes our souls and is always there for us in our Bibles. Most of all, we can ask God to use us this day according to His will, not ours.

Once, while on a weekend spiritual retreat with other women, I realized that my time alone with God had been slipping away from me, hour by hour, day by day, month by month. The theme of the retreat was developing a spiritual lifestyle, and the chosen biblical text was "Come to me, all who labor and are heavy laden, and I will give you rest" (Matthew 11:28). With a feeling of increasing sorrow, I realized that — without my intending it — time for prayer was getting a low priority in the relationships I held dear. This relationship with my Maker, the relationship that was at the heart of my being, was being shoved aside as I frantically tried to meet deadlines and serve the people who were counting on me. One sentence from that weekend is imprinted on my mind: "God will not compete with our frenzy." Of course He won't; how could we hear Him?

Making time for silence and prayerful meditation is a constant battle in our world. But to encounter God one on one, we must make time for this divine silence. While we are not mystics and may not be able to choose a deserted cave for our meditations, we can:

❋ Set aside a specific period of time every day to be alone with God in prayer. Prayer is a discipline, and our ability to pray is strengthened by our faithfulness to this discipline.

❋ Take silent walks alone in safe places — such as well-patrolled public parks — and praise God in silent prayer for the beauty we see around us.

* Let family and friends know that solitude has an important role in our spiritual development, and that when we walk silently or go off to pray we are not shutting them out but letting God in.

* Limit our exposure to the world's frenzy by carefully selecting TV programs to watch and turning on the radio only for specific reasons, not for companionship or background noise.

* Sign up for spiritual retreats that offer a respite from our busy schedules.

The Psalmist tells us that God is always there for us: "I lift up my eyes to the hills. / From whence does my help come? / My help comes from the LORD, / who made heaven and earth" (121:1-2).

He is there for us; are we there for Him?

Did You See the Cherry Trees?

Restore to me the joy of thy salvation, / and uphold me with a willing spirit. — Psalm 51:12

Our small local post office — always pokey and under-staffed — was slower than usual this morning. Two of the green laminated counters had "closed" signs on them, and one soft-spoken female postal employee was patiently trying to explain the purpose of green return postcards to an elderly man with twelve certified envelopes. He leaned closer, looking at the postcards, and the slump of his shoulders told those of us in line this would be a waiting day.

It was going to be an especially long waiting day, and the model-thin woman in line in front of me was going to be very angry, I thought. She was dressed in a white silk blouse that tied at the neck and a brown plaid suit, and she wore gold shell earrings and looked as if she had just had her grayish blond hair tinted and set at the beauty parlor.

"I hope you're not in a hurry," I said to the woman who looked like she wasn't used to waiting and might have been headed for a ladies' luncheon, bridge game, or boutique. "Coming here is a bit of a drag," I added.

The silk-shirted woman turned her coiffed head and smiled a broad smile with lips that had a freshly applied coat of glossy coral lipstick. "I'm just glad to be up and on my feet," she said. "I had major surgery not long ago, and it's so good to be out of the hospital. Did you see the cherry trees as you came in? The blossoms are so lovely this year — even prettier than last year."

My stomach did a flip-flop at the woman's unexpected cheerfulness. She must have been weak standing there in line, and there wasn't a chair or bench for customers in the post office. But she didn't say one word about how long she'd been waiting or how tired she must have felt. I didn't want to tell her I hadn't noticed the cherry trees as I came in; I'd been too busy looking down at my mail to make sure I had it all. I also didn't want to tell her I hadn't noticed the cherry trees last year either, so I couldn't compare this year's flowering to last. And I especially didn't want to tell her how ashamed I felt at considering her outing a boring chore.

I wished I hadn't called going to the post office "a drag."

On my way out of the post office on this waiting day I stopped and paused to look at the delicate pale pink cherry blossoms on the trees planted near the front door. Someone had thought to give us rushing-in, rushing-out postal customers a treat for the eyes. The least we could we do was look. As I watched, several blossoms floated down and settled on my gray jacket like spring snowflakes. They seemed to take word-form even as I watched, and that form was a flowering thank-you. *Lord,* the blossoms wanted to say to me, *thank You for people who remind us all of the sheer joy of Your creation; if we stop to listen, we find them in the most unexpected of places. And if we stop to look at what they point out to us in our haste, they can lead us ever more surely to signs of Your presence.*

Searching for Community

The red brick house sits at the top of a flight of concrete stairs, and in the spring the azaleas bloom in lush tones of deep red and the cherry tree by the front door sends its wind-driven petals showering down on us like a blessing as we walk up to ring the bell on Monday nights. We know the last step is a high one, because we've climbed it so often; we give our knees a little extra shove to get up to the stoop with its dark green door. To most neighbors, there is nothing special about this colonial house from the outside. But there is everything special about it to the eight of us.

We know the specialness of the enclosed porch with its red plaid sofa and slightly worn wooden coffee table, the table where we will spread our food, paper plates, and plastic cups for our potluck supper. We know David's cocker spaniel, Chumley, will try to lick whatever is nose-height, so we put our food up on end tables until David sends Chumley out to the backyard. We see the biblical commentary and Scripture passages waiting in a stapled pile for our discussion. And we think of the prayer requests we want to share at the end of the meeting. The comfort, the familiarity, and the hospitality are as warming as a favorite wool sweater pulled around the shoulders on a cold evening after the sun goes down.

Like many people around the world, we are rediscovering the value of banding together in small groups and meeting weekly in a home to study God's word, share fellowship, develop trust, and pray for our own needs and the needs of those close to us. We know that small groups aren't meant to substitute for regular church attendance; rather, they are a nourishing addition to worship with a church congregation. We've found that we need that nourishment as much as we need the sausages and sauerkraut Valerie brings, the lasagna Bob brings, and the stews (in the winter) and salmon-pasta salads (in the summer) I bring.

Small Christian groups are as old as the band of twelve disciples Jesus gathered about Him during the time of His ministry, but they are also as new as the face of an infant being baptized into the family of Christ. Why have we found that a small Christian group is necessary today? Quite simply because the church has grown too big to confer a sense of belonging without them, and because an increasingly secular and dehumanizing society fails to provide the support we need to practice our faith in a disciplined way.

Everyone needs to know that he or she is cared for by others. A sense of belonging is as fundamental to human beings as the need for food or shelter. Some writers have referred to this need as the need for "community." While the extended family used to confer that sense of belonging — and still does for some fortunate people — families are increasingly scattered, fractured by divorce, or weakened in other ways. Our group is no different in that respect. As families change and assume unfamiliar forms, the sense of community is eroded. Just as Christ needed His disciples about Him, so we need believers around us to strengthen us when we falter, to pray with and for us when we are in need, and to share our joys.

When members of our group travel, we pray for their safe return to us. When they or their family members are sick, we pray for their healing. We pray for the souls of those known to us who have died, and for comfort for their loved ones who remain behind. We pray for new job opportunities and for the healing of broken marriages. We pray for troubled children and teenagers having difficulty in school.

When groups of about eight members like ours come together — often from the same church or neighborhood — they find they can bond as spiritual friends, contemplate, share problems and concerns, discuss the word of God, and work together to better live out the Gospel. We've found that the small group is thus a tool for spiritual formation and a way of putting the Gospel message into action. In the group, there is usually more time for discussion and personal attention than there is in Christian education classes. The group accepts people as they are, gently challenges them to grow in a caring environment, and always confers a sense of unconditional love and acceptance. Although our small group is not a therapy group, it can help people find support for life crises such as bereavement, job loss, illness, and retirement.

A small group can also be a way of bringing the Gospel to others, as friends ask to bring friends into the group and the group grows — eventually splitting off into two groups. Those two groups, in turn, can grow and split off into four groups — and so on until the one original group can be seen as the mother group with flourishing, healthy offspring.

It would be wonderful if our faith were deepened without effort or discipline. But "just letting it happen" is not the way most of us find our faith deepening. Our faith is deepened when we connect more deeply with one another and live out our ministry with planning, study, and purpose. The people in our group have a thirst to know more about God, to read His word, discuss it with others, and probe and question in a discussion format. While sermons and theological lectures can be inspiring and enlightening, they rarely allow for the interactive communication and sharing of ideas that are at the heart of small Christian groups. We've found that give-and-take discussion helps all of us deepen our understanding of Christ's mission in an unintimidating environment and become more comfortable with the idea of witnessing to believers, those who have fallen away from the church, and the unchurched.

In our small group, members share leadership and make decisions through dialogue and consensus. Just as Jesus spurned an autocratic form of leadership, so we rely on the will of the group when making decisions about what study course to pursue or what action to take to deepen our faith. We believe that our group is an entity whose members — ourselves — are greater together than when we walk our separate paths.

✳ ✳ ✳

Our country is a nation of individualists and we like it that way. Our forebears came to this country precisely because they were individualists and could not bring themselves to conform to a way of life they did not accept.

But rugged individualism has a down side. It is lonely. It is isolating. It erects barriers between human beings. It forces people who desperately need help to pretend they don't. It stifles love.

The faces of individualism are often faces hiding pain:

✳ The bag lady sitting on a park bench clutching her few possessions to her thin chest with a scowl that says "Keep away." She is afraid if she smiles she will encourage someone to come too close, close enough to steal whatever it is she hugs to her chest.

⁂ The mother whose heart is slowly breaking because her son is using drugs and she is too scared to confront him and too proud to ask someone else for help. She is afraid if she speaks to her son about his addiction he won't love her anymore. She is afraid if she asks for counseling help, people will think she can't solve her own problems.

⁂ The widowed grandmother who lives in a retirement center far away from her children and grandchildren, and who believes they have utterly forgotten her. She has too much pride to call them on the phone and ask them to visit. *If they wanted to, they'd come,* she reasons. She is too shy to join an older singles group in her church. *They wouldn't want me,* she thinks; *I'm not witty or interesting enough to go to their meetings.*

⁂ The pregnant teenaged girl who is keeping her pregnancy a secret from everyone because she is too ashamed to reach out for help. At night, she cries silently into a wad of tissues, tossing in bed as her soul wrestles with a problem too big for her to have to handle alone.

All of these individualists have faces that, if you could see behind them, reflect the pain of not belonging.

All human beings long to belong. That is why we struggle for community in our families, churches, charitable organizations, schools, clubs, neighborhoods, offices, professional associations. That is why we celebrate birthdays, weddings, graduations, and anniversaries — and mark the deaths of loved ones. That is why we have class reunions and give people awards and certificates for achievement and meritorious service.

But still, somehow, none of it is really enough to make us feel we belong. We need to acknowledge where it is we long to go. The ultimate community is being one in the body of Christ, one with the twelve disciples who left their homes and livelihoods to follow a humble carpenter, one with the early Christian martyrs who died for their Savior. The ultimate sense of belonging is knowing Christ's love.

Jesus paid for our place in His community with His life. He bought our right to be there with His blood. That is the meaning of Easter and the resurrection. Easter means that the bag lady, the suffering mother, the abandoned grand-mother, and the pregnant teenager all belong together in the community of Christ. So does our little group of eight.

In his *Confessions*, St. Augustine wrote, "Thou, O Lord, hast made us for thyself and our hearts are restless until they rest in thee." The ultimate belonging is recognizing that Christ meant us for His own.

God Is Never Too Busy

At the ninth hour of His passion and suffering on the cross, Jesus cried out in a loud voice: "My God, my God, why hast thou forsaken me?" (Matthew 27:46; Mark 15:34). At the heart of the resurrection message is the fact that God did not desert His Son in His hour of need: He raised Jesus up in glory to sit at His side in a heavenly kingdom where pain and tears have no place.

God won't leave us, either, although sometimes it feels as if He is nowhere near.

The truth is that we leave God, He doesn't leave us. We leave Him:

* When we allow the psychological burden of past mistakes to weigh us down so heavily that we cannot look forward to the new life in Christ that is freely offered us.

* When we live in an atmosphere of despair and bitterness created by our cultivation of past hurts.

* When we busy ourselves with things, not people.

* When we forget to take the time to pray for our needs and the needs of others.

* When we ignore faces of want in our own family, circle of friends, or parish.

* When we let our lives be ruled by clock time, not by God time.

God is always available to us, if we only still our minds and hearts to be in His presence. His line is never busy, His schedule never too full to make time for us. He always keeps His appointments.

God is open to us, but the problem is that everything in our culture works to create barriers between ourselves and Him. The world values productivity, not contemplation. It is constantly there to draw us to itself, to steal our time piecemeal. It pushes and pulls. It seduces and distracts.

We would like to spend the morning reading the Bible and praying for those in need, but we have to rush out to buy groceries and go to the bank. We would like to take an hour for a quiet walk in the park to commune with God by listening to His voice in the calling of birds one to the other and observing His hand in the spring tracings of newly leafed branches against the sky, but we must sit at a desk. We must renew our car licenses, pay our taxes, wash the kitchen floor, bake two dozen cookies, fill out insurance forms, shop for new shoes, meet friends at a restaurant.

Is there anywhere in this fast-paced, clock-ruled world for time alone with God?

Leaders of contemplative prayer groups say that it is up to us to make that time; the world will not freely confer it. The world has its own agenda, and it makes no time for God. So we must make that time.

There is a place in the morning stillness between sleeping and waking when our senses belong to God time, not to clock time. There, in that early morning as our minds assume consciousness again, we can turn our thoughts to God, allow ourselves to become enveloped in and embraced by His presence. We can bring Him our thanks and our petitions and our pain. We can give Him that early morning time before the world begins to exert its clamorous claims on us. We can, if we wish, write our thoughts in a prayer diary kept on a bedside table.

Throughout the day we can program time for God. We can take a five-minute break to read from the New Testament, or to sit quietly with eyes closed. We can center ourselves with a short prayer said over and over in our heads. We can write the name of a friend in need on a piece of paper and ask God to comfort her or him throughout the day. We can from time to time mentally remove ourselves from clutter and clatter and focus our thoughts on the great joy of the resurrection: God gave Himself to us and for us in the form of His Son, and that gift is available to us today for the taking.

If you were in a desert consumed by a great thirst and someone offered you a dipper of pure water, would you refuse to drink? God is always there offering us the pure spiritual water of His love. If we refuse to reach out and take it, that is our fault, not God's.

God is never too busy for us. It is we who are too busy for Him.

The Ultimate Restoration Artist

I have my grandmother's old dining room table, a once highly varnished prize around which we gathered for Sunday dinners of turkey or ham, mashed potatoes, and my grandfather's dry comments on the news. Now the table is a worn piece with its veneer separating from its underside; the heirloom holds piles of my papers in ragtag stacks begging to be sorted, for like most of us I'm drowning in the deluge of paper that comes through my front mail drop.

My grandmother's table is badly in need of a wood-restoration expert, and I've been meaning to try to find one in the Yellow Pages. In our world of imperfection, restoration artists abound, and I'm certain they're listed there along with car dealers, house painters, and Oriental-rug sellers. We can take our chipped, gouged, and nicked tables and chairs to furniture restorers who use special tools and waxes. We can take our faded, tattered old family portraits to photograph restorers who use darkroom and touch-up techniques to give us whole faces. We can have old silver replated, and ancestral paintings refurbished by restoration artists who work with delicate brushes and carefully mixed oils.

As I was using Elmer's Glue to try to make that separated piece of veneer lie flat (it didn't work), I thought about a tougher challenge: where to take broken souls in need of restoration. The Easter message gives us a very clear answer on that: Jesus is the great lover and restorer of human souls. He'll take them whatever their condition, and the sign on His restoration shop always says "open."

The restoration message goes back to the early days of humankind, before a carpenter in Nazareth came to put things right with the spiritual tools He needed for the job. The story of Genesis is the tale of a good work sullied, a bountiful ecosystem put awry by human sin. In the story of temptation in the garden of Eden, we see that from the very earliest times — the days of the prototype man and woman — humankind followed wayward actions that separate us from God.

Surely that tree with its forbidden fruit was just too tempting. Had we been there, would we have been able to resist its shiny plumpness? From the time of Adam and Eve, human beings in all generations have had to endure the consequences of misunderstanding, chaos, violence, and suffering that are the hallmarks of a broken relationship with God and with one another.

Even the best of human relationships is marred by that brokenness. When a close friend says, "Tell me honestly what you think" and you do, chances are it will be misunderstood. She doesn't really want to hear what you think; she wants to hear something she's scripted in her mind.

Into this world of brokenness and human imperfection came the ultimate restorer. His was not the pretty task of resilvering a Georgian tray or touching up the pink cheeks of an eighteenth-century noblewoman. His was the arduous task of bringing human beings back into a right relationship with their Maker. To complete this task, the Son of Man had to take on Himself the sins of the world, a phrase that conjures up a ponderous, weighted sack full of all the dark evils that weigh humankind down. We couldn't carry it, since it was much too heavy even to drag. By willingly accepting the baggage and the way of the cross, Jesus put Himself in our place and even felt abandoned by His loving Father. This acceptance of the pain of total abandonment for our sake was His ultimate sacrifice. Only this ultimate sacrifice could buy the ultimate restoration.

Think of the carpenter using his tools to fit intricate pieces of wood together. This image makes Jesus' gifts in spiritual restoration more concrete. Shave a little here, build up this side to match the height of the other . . .

Jesus' resurrection from death and defeat is a triumph for humankind because when God welcomed back His beloved Son, He welcomed us back, too, chastened children in need of love and family. Jesus does not ask us to follow His way on the cross. That walk was for Him to take, and it was to be done only once in history. What Jesus asks is that we take up our own life crosses, whatever they may be, and carry them willingly in His name. He asks us to carry grief, physical and mental handicaps, betrayal by friends, the care of a helpless relative, poverty, illness, loneliness, abuse, and all the burdens of being fully human. He simply asks us not to run away from or to disown these aspects of humanness in our broken world, but to accept them, live with them, and carry them as best we can in humility and charity.

Unlike Jesus, we do not need to feel the pain of utter abandonment as we bear the crosses of this life. We have a companion in our suffering, the spiritual best friend who went before us on His own cross to prepare our way with the Father. We have a loving source of comfort who walked the way, who understands the heart's pain. While this companionship does not take away our pain, it makes the pain possible to bear.

And thus we have the Easter paradox: Take up your burden and your load will be lightened. Bear your cross and you will find it easier to carry than if you put it down.

I think Jesus wanted us to know that the alternative to ignoring the gift of the ultimate restorer is alienation from God. He wanted to save us from the torment and guilt that alienation brings. He must have known that the load of a heavy conscience can be a far greater burden to bear than the load of a life lived in an honest attempt to follow His own gentle directives. I know a man who hasn't spoken to his son in ten years because he can't bring himself to forgive and neither can the son. They argued over the son's drug habit, words were hurled like rocks, and they walked away from each other. Neither one will take that first step back, and the fact that he can't, or won't, torments the father and makes his face drawn and the corners of his mouth sag. "Come to me, all who labor and are heavy laden, and I will give you rest" (Matthew 11:28) is an invitation to put our souls into the loving hands of the ultimate restoration artist, trusting that He will do with us what is needed to bring us back to God — shaving a little here and building up a little there to make us stand more evenly.

We are all spiritual works in progress. We are all broken and sinful. There is not one of us who does not need restoration to bring us back to the place of the soul where we can be in harmony with our Father. It takes more than the spiritual equivalent of Elmer's Glue. Jesus did His part by choosing and following the way of the cross. No one made Him do it; it was a free offering of grace.

When we follow our own way of the cross, choosing our steps carefully, picking our way over stones, we are working in partnership with Jesus to complete our spiritual restoration. We are working toward that day when we recognize that it is only by the mercy of the ultimate restorer that we can come back to our rightful home with our rightful Father.

Filling Our Spiritual Lamps

Like many homeless people in the nation's capital, the man on my left was talking out loud as he strode rapidly with arms swinging along K Street near its intersection with Connecticut Avenue, corridor of law firms and trade associations. Sockless in graying white jogging shoes, dressed in a dirt-smudged maroon-and-gold Redskins sweatshirt and jeans, the man was talking about the second coming of Christ.

"Sweet Jesus, oh, He's coming," he said loudly, smiling broadly and looking straight ahead as he walked along swinging his arms. "Yes, Lord, You're coming now and I know it!" he yelled, his voice rising to an octave higher on "know it." The men in dark gray and blue suits moved their briefcases nearer their bodies, but did not turn their heads toward him. Neither did most of us women in our tailored suits with matching skirts that ended just above the knee, hugging our shoulder purses more closely. We were picking our way carefully on shoes with squared toes and thick heels, for we succumbed to style.

The homeless man paid us no heed. Looking ahead at something we couldn't see, he laughed aloud and called out his message as he passed the street vendors with their covered stalls of imported scarves, perfume, ties, and leather purses. "Oh, sweet Jesus, coming for you and me," he yelled, as he approached Sixteenth Street. And there I lost the homeless man in the Redskins sweatshirt, for he was going too fast for me.

What would he have said if I'd stopped him and tried to talk to him? Would he have given me a specific day of Jesus' coming, an hour? Would he have spat in my face or even heard my question reverberating in the mental house he had constructed for himself? If he had answered and told me exactly when to expect Jesus, would I have believed him? Because I didn't ask, I don't know the answers to any of these questions.

But there are clues to the homeless man's message in the Bible. Jesus was the master storyteller, the man whose carefully crafted parables always packed a special punch for those who had ears to hear. So it was with the story of the ten maidens who picked up their lamps and went out to meet their bridegroom (see Matthew 25:1-13).

This is a story about the coming of the kingdom of God rooted in culture and custom, for in the Palestinian tradition a bridegroom came and fetched his bride from her parents' home to his own. As Matthew tells us, five of these young women were unprepared, and took no extra oil for their oil-burning lamps when they went out joyfully to meet the bridegroom. But the other five women were wise, and carried extra flasks of oil along with their lamps.

When the bridegroom was delayed, all ten maidens yielded to their heavy-lidded temptation to sleep, and thus they were slumbering when he arrived at midnight. Upon hearing the excited cry — "Behold the bridegroom! Come out to meet him!" — all ten young women rubbed the remnants of sleep from their eyes, rose quickly, and went out with quick and eager steps, trimming their oil lamps to light their way. But, predictably, the lamps of the five unprepared maidens went out, and the five wise ones refused to share their oil for fear they would not have enough. Thus the five foolish young women scurried off to buy more oil in the market, and when they returned the other five were enjoying a marriage feast behind a door that was barred.

At the end of this parable, Matthew warns, "Watch, therefore, for you know neither the day nor the hour."

My homeless friend seems to know more about this parable than all of us in dark business suits and short skirts walking along K Street, for there is a clear call to action behind this warning. What the homeless man seems to know is that the kingdom of God is now, not at some far-off time. He seems to know that the Jesus He expects can approach him on K Street at any time, saying, "See, I was with you all the time." A turn of the head, a look of the eyes: The homeless man proclaiming his message would know Jesus if he saw Him.

But, because I did not speak, I might not be there when Jesus comes. I might not know Him. The Bridegroom calls us all — hungry or well-fed, housed or homeless, silent or yelling, well or sick, churched or unchurched — to His feast at this very hour.

Are our lamps really lit with light-giving oil for Jesus, or do they need a little tending? Do we honor and recognize Him in the person of the homeless man striding along proclaiming His second coming, the shut-in battling brain cancer alone, the bereaved widow and children trying to put the pieces of their shattered lives back together without the one who always provided the glue? Are we there to provide food, time, ears to listen, words of comfort?

I think what Jesus wanted to say is that for those who seek it, the marriage feast of salvation is always prepared and ready. The homeless man on K Street seemed to know that truth despite — or maybe because of — his poverty. If we are close to Jesus, we can share in that abundant banquet right now. But for us to be ready for that heavenly feast, we need to be constantly vigilant about our state of preparedness. Is that spiritual lamp getting a little low, its oil used up by discouragement, unresolved anger, broken relationships. . . ?

Are we filling our lamps with the fuel of prayer and God's word, or do we put off intimate time with Him because He has too many secular competitors? Are we filling our lamps with true generosity when we give ourselves to others, or are we hoarding parts of ourselves tightly like psychic misers? Are we filling our lamps with reverence for the holy temples of our bodies, eating in moderation, getting enough sleep and exercise? Do we fill those lamps with our recognition of and response to the face of Christ in those closest to us and those we meet as strangers?

Being spiritually prepared for the bridegroom's coming was not a difficult task for the five wise young women who had enough oil to light their way to his side. Evidently they had been laying up enough of a supply of oil to be ready for the moment of his arrival. They had no doubt been watching their supply of oil every day, checking its level, replenishing it when their flasks were low, and tending their lamps with care.

But somehow the five foolish young women had gotten off track. Maybe they were distracted with other duties: cooking, sewing, taking care of younger siblings. Maybe they were dreamers, planning for a future they endowed with grandiose expectations of what marriage would be like. Maybe they were too busy sharing their hopes with one another, chattering excitedly about their wedding dresses, their jewelry, and their dowries.

Whatever the reason, five women were ready for Jesus and five weren't.

I would have liked to ask the homeless man what he did to stay ready. I would have liked to ask him where he got the oil for his spiritual lamp, for oil is so very expensive and he seemed not to have a nickel. I would have liked to have given him something, but I didn't know what to give him that he didn't already have.

Whatever he had, the homeless man on K Street seemed to know that the Bridegroom calls us even now to the marriage feast.

Part 4

*Godly Glimpses
in Daily Service*

Seeing with the Heart

Condemned as a sinner and an outcast, the woman stiffened her spine against the catcalls and jeers she knew she would hear as she worked her way inside the Pharisee's house with her alabaster jar to find Jesus, who had gone there to eat. Living in the shadows as she did, it must have taken great courage to go into that house; she might have been beaten or stoned.

She stood behind Jesus, weeping, and began to wash His feet with her stream of tears and dry the skin of His weary feet with her long hair. How good this must have felt to Jesus, a nomadic teacher in a dry and thirsty land where dust layered everything, especially feet. The woman began kissing Jesus' feet and anointing them with the precious, costly ointment she had brought in her alabaster jar. Her kisses and her tears and the ointment mingled on His skin and soothed Jesus' feet and His heart. Her tenderness was like the touch of the most caring mother, and her deep yearning for forgiveness touched His soul as surely as her hands touched His feet.

But the Pharisee, a man, saw none of this. Indeed, he was quietly outraged that the rabbi tolerated the woman, and muttered to himself that a real prophet would have known the woman was a sinner, would have repudiated her touch, and would have cast her off. Were not Pharisees trained in the law of the God of Israel? Sinners were to be condemned. The Pharisee saw none of the tenderness of this moment of tears and touch because he could not see with his heart; his heart was too hard. And thus he missed the entire point of the incident of the woman who bathed Jesus' feet with her tears: We are all sinners and we all need forgiveness, even Pharisees. Especially Pharisees. She knew she was a sinner and needed God's healing love; the Pharisee didn't. It was the woman with the alabaster jar who saw how close to the heart of God Jesus was, not the Pharisee. For all his scriptural learning, honors, and community standing, the Pharisee was an outcast when it came to seeing what the woman did. And so it was she who received forgiveness from Jesus, and the Pharisee who incurred the master's rebuke.

Blessed are women who, like the woman at Jesus' feet,

can see with the heart. For they are the ones who see truly. (See Luke 7:36-50.)

※ ※ ※

In a remarkable letter to the women of the world dated June 29, 1995, Pope John Paul II thanked us for our contributions to humanity, placing special emphasis on our ability to see people with our hearts. The pope said, "Perhaps more than men, women acknowledge the person, because they see persons with their hearts."

What does it mean to see others with the heart? In his twelve-point letter, the pontiff states that women see people "independently of various ideological or political systems. They see others in their greatness and limitations; they try to go out to them and help them." Seeing with the heart, then, is the ability to perceive and celebrate the worth of each individual God created, recognizing that however unlovable that person may sometimes seem, he or she was created in His likeness. Seeing with the heart is a commitment to serve as well as to see.

The pope's "Letter to Women," written before the historic United Nations' Fourth World Conference on Women held in Beijing, China, is all the more significant because it was written by a man and the head of a powerful Church. It is a courageous and ultimately humble attempt to praise women for their unique contributions. The letter even contains an apology to women for the wrongs society has done them: marginalization and servitude, emanating even from within the Church, sexual exploitation and discrimination.

In thanking women for their ability to see with the heart, the pontiff tackles an area of raging controversy: gender equality. Noting that "progress usually tends to be measured according to the criteria of science and technology," he first pays tribute to women who made contributions in these fields. It was Marie (née Sklodowska) Curie, after all — Polish like the pope himself — who received the Nobel prize in chemistry in 1911 for her discovery of radium. But John Paul II then goes on to say that technological advancement is "not the only measure of progress, nor in fact is it the principal one."

Rather, writes the pope, women's unique contributions have been most notable in the "social and ethical dimension, which deals with human relations and spiritual values." In this area of often unsung daily service to others, he believes the "genius of women" has been most in evidence. The pontiff cites day-to-day relationships with people, especially within the family, but also in the field of education beyond the family: nurseries, schools, universities, social service agencies, parishes, associations, and societal movements of various kinds.

In serving others through human relationships — especially the weakest and most defenseless — women "exhibit a kind of affective, cultural and spiritual motherhood which has inestimable value for the development of individuals and the future of society," writes Pope John Paul II.

The message of this papal letter is that women are the torchbearers of a form of knowing that has just as much validity as science. When we women accept and internalize others' denigration of our gift of seeing with the heart, we betray that gift and reject it as we would reject an unruly weed in an ordered garden. Conversely, when we embrace this form of knowing, we are better able to serve a world that can use our special gift of sight. We are better able to give ourselves to relationships, work, prayer, and the arts. By using our glimpses of what we see with the heart, we can exercise our spontaneity and creativity in the most freeing and energizing of ways.

So seeing with the heart is not something we need to be ashamed of — as if it marked us somehow as emotional or irrational. Rather, seeing with the heart is a gift from God, a gift to be freely used and celebrated with joy and thanks to our Creator. We don't have to be apologetic about this special insight — which is often called "women's intuition" in a derogatory way and put down by a male-dominated society. Our intuitive gifts help us raise children, be good wives, serve our parishes, work in various occupations, and give many volunteer hours to those who can't help themselves.

How refreshing this message is. In an era that places so much emphasis on the rational, scientific, and technical, on physics and the laws of cause and effect, it is heartening to hear that our special gifts have much value in the world. It is heartening to hear from the pope himself that seeing with the heart is an ability to be commended, cherished, honored, and cultivated.

Noting that "Jesus treated women with openness, respect, acceptance and tenderness," the pontiff states: "Womanhood expresses the 'human' as much as manhood does, but in a different and complementary way."

Whatever way it is, that complementary way, it allows us to see with the heart. It allows us to see with our hearts into the hearts of others, and by seeing what needs doing, we can do the work God meant us to do.

Ashes on the Head, Flame in the Heart

Walking out of my church on Ash Wednesday, I purposely left the smudge of ashes on my forehead. In years past, I had wiped the cross-shaped mark off before shopping or doing errands, but not this year. This year it seemed important to have some outward sign of this significant day on the church calendar, this day when we remember that we are dust.

Why?

Maybe it was because I had seen the tall, strong bodies of my two husbands reduced to ash, just a small amount of ash that would fit in a box and could be scattered in a grave, and I wanted the ashes on my forehead to symbolize my connection with them. Remember that "you are dust, / and to dust you shall return" (Genesis 3:19). Maybe it was because my small Scripture study group had been talking about the importance of witnessing to our faith, and I wanted the cross-shaped mark to be a witness. Maybe it was because I wanted those I met to be reminded of Lent, that quiet time before the glorious resurrection when we look deeply inside ourselves in preparation for the holy mystery of Easter. Maybe it was all of these things.

In the local city grocery store, the man behind the delicatessen counter said, "Oh, it's Ash Wednesday," as I bought some home-style potato salad. Did I only imagine it, or was there a hint of guilt in his comment? I did not want these ashes on my head to make anyone feel guilty. Was he thinking that he should have gone to church? Was he thinking that there was still time, that he could still go?

"Yes," I said, smiling, "it's Ash Wednesday." I thanked him for the potato salad, trying to be especially appreciative in the way I smiled and reached for the plastic container. "It looks very good," I said. "Everything I've tried from your deli tastes good."

The deli man beamed, all traces of guilt gone from his face. "We try," he said.

Pushing my grocery cart down the aisles, I saw people giving me sidelong glances. Did they know what the ashes meant? Were some of them thinking I needed to wash my face? I smiled at each person I saw. I pulled my cart out of the way for one mother whose child was reaching for a cereal box, helped an elderly woman reach a cake mix on a high upper shelf. I purposely let someone get ahead of me in the checkout line. I handed a store coupon for bread I'd received in the mail to a man who looked as if he could use it. I smiled at all these people in this city grocery, and — after looking at the ash mark — they all smiled back. No one but the deli man commented on what the ashes meant, although I thought some people wanted to speak.

Outside the store, spring was trying to chase a cold, rainy March out of our city for good. The sky was trying hard to turn from gray to blue. A breeze with a new softness in its stroke blew across the parking lot, and the attendant turned his face up toward it, pausing before loading bags in a white minivan. He looked at me, saw the ashes, and then smiled across the grocery cart.

"I'll carry today," I said.

"Are you sure?" he answered. Then, "Spring's coming."

"It is for sure," I replied, smiling back. Yes, spring was coming, with its glorious, passionate burst of colors. Yellows and oranges that leaped from the green grass like flame. And then I thought of another meaning for those ashes on my head. I had always thought of them as the dust of death, the mark of mortality, the sign of sin and decay; but ashes are also the remnant of fire. Ashes are the end result of flames that once burned brightly, as Christ's heart did for us and as He wants our hearts to do for Him. It was that burning in His heart that drove Jesus to sacrifice Himself to redeem our sins, and that propelled Him up on the cross to die ignominiously with common criminals.

This year I did not feel diminished, saddened, or deadened by this mark of ash on my head; in some strange way I felt energized, lightened, empowered to go out of my way to be kind in small ways in that city grocery. Although the Ash Wednesday service had been sobering, with its emphasis on prayer, fasting, self-denial, and repentance, this year there seemed nothing doleful about the service. Instead, it seemed freeing. It seemed an invitation to shed what didn't really matter, embrace simplicity, and concentrate on tending that flame of service to the Lord, the flame that burns in the heart, where it needs daily fanning. *All glory and honor to God, for in the blood of Christ He has ratified a new and everlasting covenant with His people, and renews it in the sacrament of the altar.**

The ashes on our heads on Ash Wednesday are a symbol not only of our mortality but also of what our hearts should be doing: burning with love for God and our neighbor. If our hearts are not burning with that flame of love that turns to ash only when we die, then it is time to spend some time during Lent contemplating why and asking for forgiveness. *The time of penance has come, the time to atone for our sins and to seek our salvation.**

Has the flame burned low because we became immersed in our own projects, to the exclusion of others' needs? Have we forgotten to fan the fire of our love for God and neighbor because we were fanning another fire, the fire of our own desires? Has the fire that burns for God almost gone out because we have forgotten our call to serve? Have we inadvertently and unintentionally been self-indulgent, full of pride, hypocritical, impatient, exploitative of others, angry, jealous, greedy, or negligent? *Create in me a clean heart, O God. / and put a new and right spirit within me.* — Psalm 51:10

Lord, it was You who lit the fire inside us to begin with, and it is only You who can put it out at the end. These ashes are Your mark, Your outward sign that we belong to You and to You we shall return. So while we have life and breath and strength, help us tend that fire in the heart and fan its flames, for it burns only for You.

---

*Excerpted from *Christian Prayer: The Liturgy of the Hours*, Daughters of St. Paul, St. Paul's Editions, 1976.

Lord of Another Chance

There is something noble about human beings surpassing themselves.

In today's newspaper, we read of a man plunging into a river to pull a toddler out before she drowns, the child's pink overalls sodden, one small sneaker left down on the squishy bottom of those murky waters that claim the lives of people hapless enough to slide down the river's slippery banks of thriving, water-nourished grass. The sneaker will rot, but the little girl will recover; the newspaper photo shows the mother reaching out for her child as the hero clutches the wet saved bundle to his chest.

By trade the man is an electrician, more used to splicing wires and tracing intricate electrical connections than plunging into rivers to save children. He disclaims all notions of heroism: "I did what anybody would have done." But we make him into a hero anyway, and we will see his picture again, receiving a mayor's award for bravery, uncomfortable in the suit and the tie he bought for this occasion and may not wear again unless he puts it on for church.

This is the age of superheroes. We live in a competitive era that glorifies winners who take their one chance in life, go for it, and succeed. We bestow today's versions of laurel wreaths on the football player who makes the winning kick at just the right moment, to a crescendo of cheers; on the unknown actress chosen by a celebrated movie director for an ingenue's dream role who becomes a star overnight; on the unknown and unseeded teenager who survives to the semifinals and then makes it to the finals at Wimbledon, winning the world's most prestigious tennis tournament with an ace of a serve that's clocked at one hundred twenty-five miles per hour.

We glorify the superhuman reserves required to be a winner under extreme pressure. Everyone lauds a hero or heroine. Everyone praises life's Olympic medalists who push themselves beyond endurance and succeed. We cheer past the lump in our throats as the skater in her black-and-red confection of a dress lands two triple jumps in succession to the escalating strains of Ravel's *Boléro*. We cry along with the rest, tears of joy forming in our eyes for that bright young star newly created in one exploding burst of muscle-tensing, bone-stretching, and mind-bending effort.

But what happens when the football player misses the kick? When the unknown actress is passed over at the final audition for someone with more experience? When the electrician swims as hard as he can, but the river's frothy churning current pulls the child in her sodden pink overalls away from the man's grasp and down to her death with the small sneaker lying on the squishy bottom? When the young skater in frilly red and black misses her second triple and lands directly on her backside?

In our culture of instant winners, these people have failed and been made instant has-beens because they missed their moment of opportunity. The football player is a loser to be jeered, the actress has lost her once-in-a-lifetime chance at the brass ring of stardom, the electrician is consigned to self-recrimination and the pain of "what-ifs," and the ice skater seriously considers giving up the dream that smoldered inside her, getting her out of bed at five o'clock morning after dark morning.

They are has-beens unless they turn to the message of Christ.

Jesus is lord of the second chance, and the third, and the fourth . . . and another and another. He keeps giving all of us another try, a chance to do better, to be better, to live a new life in Him. Lover of souls who stumble and falter and sin, Jesus keeps picking us up, dusting us off, and salving our bruised egos with His love.

The graphic biblical example of the restorative second chance is Pentecost, day of signs and wonders, day of a rushing sound like the roar of wind and tongues of flame that turned the bemused disciples into articulate linguists. Imagine the apostles after Jesus' crucifixion: a ragtag bunch of demoralized men who thought their world had ended. They had lost their leader in an ignominious death on the cross; they feared for their lives and wanted to hide; and Peter, rock on whom the new Church was to be built, was still struggling with a burden of guilt at his betrayal of his master.

If ever anyone needed another chance, it was that little group of Jesus' followers. If ever anyone doubted whether he could carry on at all, let alone spread the Gospel of Christ, it was Peter, sitting with head drooping among the disciples, unable to summon the reserves of strength needed to empower this small band to carry on their master's work. *When the day of Pentecost had come, they were all together in one place. And suddenly a sound came from heaven like the rush of a mighty wind, and it filled all the house where they were sitting. And there appeared to them tongues as of fire, distributed and resting on each one of them. And they were all filled with the Holy Spirit and began to speak in other tongues, as the Spirit gave them utterance.* — Acts 2:1-4

And so the rush of sound like wind that blew the power of the Holy Spirit into the newly created Church also blew the hope of new life into the disciples and gave them a second chance. At last they could understand fully that everything Christ had said to them was true. He had risen from the dead, and had shown Himself to them following His death. As the Acts of the Apostles (1:8) points out, Jesus had not left them comfortless, and had brought a new source of support to them: *You shall receive power when the Holy Spirit has come upon you; and you shall be my witnesses in Jerusalem and in all Judea and Samaria and to the end of the earth.* Jesus had given a sorrowful, dispirited, weakened group of men new life in Him, and a heartened resolve to spread His word to those who did not know Him.

Being given another chance at abundant life is a gift more precious than any accolades we can receive as earthly winners. It beats having our picture taken with the mayor or winning Wimbledon or having the gold medal placed around our neck at the Olympic games. Being given another chance means that no matter what we do or how far we have fallen from grace in society's or our own eyes, Jesus will take us back. He will not spurn us as has-beens. He will not reject us for the team or berate us for failing to pass a test. He will never jeer, turn his back, or call us names. When we turn to Him in our woundedness and our need, He will always enfold us to Himself.

When Jesus blessed and commissioned the disciples at Pentecost, He accepted us into this new, ongoing life of spiritual empowerment as well. We are no longer frail creatures dependent upon our own limited abilities — oxygen-deprived muscles straining, minds concentrated to the point where stress becomes the only reality — and trapped by our failures, but gifted inheritors of the kingdom of God. Along with Peter, we can rejoice that the strength Jesus imparted to the disciples with the Holy Spirit has also been given to us as representatives of the body of Christ on earth. Like Peter, we always have another chance.

Accessible Worship for All

I was glad when they said to me, / "Let us go to the house of the LORD!" — Psalm 122:1

The elderly woman, who might have been eighty-five, leaned on her cane and looked ahead to the tall flight of steps leading to the imposing old stone church with its massive double doors crowned by a round stained-glass medallion window.

She and I had come to this church — where I had never been before — to attend an evening concert of opera selections. I was there specifically to hear my sixteen-year-old nephew, Christopher, sing with his high school chorus, which had been honored with an invitation to perform as a prelude to the professionals. I could see the woman, a stranger to me, assessing the distance to the steps across a stone courtyard, considering their height and number, and deciding whether she would have the energy to make it all the way up.

On this windy Saturday evening, I wanted to leave my family and go up to the woman and take her elbow, but I was afraid her pride would stand in the way of both of us. I opted to preserve the pride, but to follow behind the woman at a short distance as she walked across the courtyard and up the steps — haltingly, the cane tapping, pausing to lean on the iron railing and take breaths. I wouldn't hurt her pride, I reasoned, if I stayed behind her to catch her if she should stumble and start to tilt backward.

At the top of the flight of steps, the woman paused and leaned on her cane as people elbowed past her at the crowded entrance to the massive doors, anxious to get good seats for the show. I edged up to the woman, making sure I was there to help hold open one of the doors when she went through. There seemed to be no one stationed at the door to do this; people shouldered through and — unless held — the heavy door swung back, its weight a solid barrier against entry to all but the physically strong.

Once inside, I went to look for a rest room. Following a sign, I started down a long, steep flight of steps. "Excuse me," I said to someone on his way up. "Is there an elevator in this church?"

He shrugged. "I don't believe so," he said. I was thinking not of myself, but of the elderly woman with the cane. How could she go to the bathroom if she needed to do so? I asked some more people about an elevator. The answers were no and no and no.

Now I was beginning to feel angry, and my feet seemed to stomp on that steep staircase on the way back up. Wasn't a church supposed to welcome the infirm as well as the able-bodied? Wasn't a church supposed to be for those who used canes and walkers and wheelchairs as well as those who could, like my nephew, Christopher, race down a soccer field to make a goal? Still angry on behalf of the woman with the cane, I found my way to my family.

I listened to the young, pure voices of Christopher's high school chorus. As they sang "Who'll be a witness for my Lord?" I tried to let the words of this traditional spiritual, "Witness," block out the uncharitable thoughts I was having toward the members of this church, people I didn't even know. Where was the witness in this church? Didn't they know about the Americans with Disabilities Act? Why hadn't they made more of an effort to make the aged and disabled feel more welcome? What message were they sending with the imposing flight of stairs outside (and no ramp that I could see) and the steep stairs inside to the rest rooms (and no elevator)?

The opera selections began, and as I listened I read the words of "Va, Pensiero," from Verdi's *Nabucco*: "Wings of gold, take my thoughts filled with longing far away to my home among the mountains. . . ." This church didn't provide wings of gold; it didn't even provide an elevator to the rest room.

I thought of an incident in my own church, when I had stood just inside the double doors (also heavy) on a raw Sunday evening, waiting for a knock on the outside to signal me to open one of the large doors for a wheelchair. A young girl was bringing her elderly grandmother up the outside ramp to a church concert. At least there was a ramp. But who was supposed to open the door?

Several of us helped the young girl — whose face was set in lines of worry that didn't go with her youth — maneuver the wheelchair through the doors and into the church. As she thanked us, the white-haired grandmother sitting in the chair turned to me, gave me a very small smile (as if she wasn't allowed), and said, "I'm sorry to be such a bother." A bother? Simply because she wanted to come to church? I hoped my smile and reassuring words conveyed welcome. But the big double doors that swung shut if not held by someone strong did not.

Now the professional chorus and a guest mezzo-soprano were singing "Regina Coeli," the Easter hymn from Mascagni's *Cavalleria Rusticana*. Somehow, I wasn't in the right Easter mood to hear this transcendent music, but I read the words in the choral text in the program anyway: "Hail, Queen of heaven, all glorious. Alleluia. Thy son is risen victorious, whom the Lord chose thee as worthy to bear. O sing praise to the Lord who is risen, Death's dominion and power to deny; he has broken the bonds of his prison, he is risen to glory on high!" What would Jesus think of the barriers of this church, He who broke the bonds of civility and circumstance and ministered to paralytics, lepers, the blind, and those with demons screaming inside them?

There was so much we all could have done better. As Christians, we wanted to believe we treated people with disabilities just like us. But as human beings we found it difficult to overlook even the most minor differences in our neighbors. How then to overlook a wheelchair? Crutches? A leg brace? A facial expression that signals retardation? Even a cane? Maybe I should have gone up to the older woman with the cane and spoken to her, not to offer help but just to be friendly. Maybe I should have invited her to sit with my family, since she seemed to be alone. Maybe if I had asked her to join us I could have carried her concert program for her and helped her get seated. No one else seemed to be doing it. But, of course, the members of this church hadn't even thought it important to put in an elevator to the rest rooms.

It was hard to feel triumphant during the triumphal march from Verdi's *Aida* that closed the concert, even though the trumpet and the voices from combined choruses — including Christopher's high school group — filled the large church with music to shake the rafters and rattle the stained-glass medallion window over the front doors. I was still thinking of the older woman with the cane. Was she needing to go the bathroom? Could she get down the steps? Could she get back up?

How long would it take her? What if she fell forward on the way down or backward on the way up?

As we walked out into the vestibule of the church to find Christopher and congratulate him, I saw a table of brochures. My eyes scanned the title of one and I stopped and drew in a breath.

"Making our church accessible to all," I read on the front. I picked up the brochure and started to read, my anger on behalf of the woman with the cane fizzling out with the words the congregation had written in love. As I read, all I wanted now was to say "I'm sorry" to the members of this church for the thoughts I had been thinking during the concert.

I read: "Inspired by the Word and Spirit, we now have a plan that brings down the barriers. This plan will allow all to participate in our worship and life as a congregation and will bring our buildings up to modern standards of accessibility." I read about a wheelchair-accessible ramp, an elevator, a new wheelchair-accessible family rest room, a handicapped parking area and sidewalks to accessible church entrances. I read that the church would need about half a million dollars to make these changes, and that they had started a fund drive called Accessible Worship Now.

As I read the words the members of this church had written, I felt very small and very flawed. My negative thoughts had been just as disabling as the lameness that caused someone to use a cane. They had prevented me from experiencing the joyous sounds of the operatic music to the fullest. "We will need to move with confidence in God's blessings," I read in the brochure. "Let us embrace the possibilities and accept the challenge, trusting that with God all things are possible, and responding in love to the hurts and hopes of all people, inviting others to join and celebrate the journey of faith."

I would ask God for forgiveness for the uncharitable thoughts I had been thinking. I would try to pray in simple words, words that went something like this: "Lord, when we are handicapped by hasty judgment of others — or indeed by any judgment at all — cleanse our hearts of harsh feelings and give us the wisdom and patience to hold our mental tongues and think the best of them. And as we cannot do this by ourselves, please empower us with Your love, which always seeks the good that is in everyone." I would pray hard, for I had been very unkind.

Yes, I would pray for forgiveness for those uncharitable, handicapping thoughts. And I would send a contribution to the Accessible Worship Now fund drive.

The Telephone Miracle

Blessed are the peacemakers, for they will be called children of God. — Matthew 5:9, *New American Bible*

The timing of the call about my eighty-six-year-old mother-in-law's medical crisis could not have been worse. I was struggling to cope with a variety of personal problems and business decisions, and I was trying to keep my challenging career going, too. I was house-sitting for my vacationing parents, and the responsibility of looking after this older home — once my girlhood home — was weighing on my shoulders.

But my father-in-law's voice — when he could speak — demanded my attention, and over the phone lines from his home in Florida to my parents' home in Maryland, I could feel his emotional turmoil in the pit of my own stomach. As calmly as I could, I questioned Opa, as I called him, and learned that Oma — my mother-in-law — needed a second operation as soon as possible. She had been operated on for an intestinal disorder called diverticulosis only days before, and now she was bleeding internally from an ulcer. At eighty-six, her wracked body could hardly take more surgery; yet if she didn't have the operation she would hemorrhage and die.

But, I learned, she was refusing more surgery. Worse, Opa and the surgeon had had a disagreement and had exchanged harsh words, and now this medical expert was threatening to walk off the case just when he was most needed.

I sat there with the phone in my hand, my head reeling as thoughts scattered themselves in my brain in no particular order. Should I drop everything I was doing, leave my affairs untended, and go to Florida to be there at my mother-in-law's side? I had not been able to bring myself to get on an airplane since my husband Jim's death in a plane crash. Could I take a train? Would Oma have the surgery if I asked her to? Would my presence make any difference at all?

I had the number of the nursing station near the intensive care unit in the Florida hospital where Oma was recovering from her first operation, and I dialed it with trembling hands. "Just a minute," said the nurse, when I identified myself, "I'll let you talk to your mother-in-law yourself. I have

a special hookup. Be sure to speak up so she can hear you."
A phone in intensive care? How had the nurse managed this
small miracle?

"Oma," I said distinctly, not even conscious of what was
coming out, "I'm coming down . . . you have to have the operation . . . I love you . . . please hang on until I get there."

Her voice was weak, but I could hear her well. "Oh, Peggy,"
she said, "it's so good to hear you." That was all I needed to
get on the train.

My mother-in-law was operated on while I was on the
Amtrak train from Washington, D.C., to Tampa, Florida, and
recovered well. In fact, she said she felt better after the operation than she had in years.

I learned that it was the nurse of the telephone miracle
who helped smooth the situation with Opa and the doctor.
The nurse very quietly and skillfully stroked bruised egos,
delivered pep talks, held my mother-in-law's hand in hers. I
believe she was responsible for saving Oma's life.

In mysterious ways, God continues to guide and
strengthen peacemakers in all walks of life, whether they serve
Him in hospitals, churches, families, schools, or legislative
offices. Every day, these peacemakers smooth ruffled feelings, mend broken relationships, and keep the wheels of human interaction turning. Their names aren't in the paper,
usually, and the small miracles they work don't get on TV.
But they are miracles nonetheless.

In my case, the nurse of the telephone miracle came by
her talents as a peacemaker naturally. Her name was Mary.

Jesus' Most Precious Gift

When a close friend extended and then withdrew an invitation, I felt hurt, betrayed, and rejected. As my eyes filled with tears, I thought about my feelings and tried to analyze them. Then I tried to think how the truly rejected people in our society must feel.

What could feel worse in the depths of a human soul than knowing you are unwanted? Pediatric nurses have long known that babies in orphanages die from a soul sickness called failure-to-thrive if they are not held and cuddled — even when all their bodily needs are met. The hunger for human love is stronger than that for milk, for warmth, for dry clothes, for sleep.

What the child Jesus brought to us was God's unconditional love, the gift of acceptance. Isn't this the most precious gift of all, and the key to Christianity's global appeal? It means that no matter what our past sins, no matter what our faults, no matter how we have offended God and others, if we turn to Him with truly penitent hearts and ask forgiveness — right now — God will welcome us as His beloved children. The way to this New Testament God — the God of forgiveness — is through Jesus, whose birth marked a new covenant of love between God and humankind.

Consider what this priceless gift of being wanted and loved unconditionally could mean to:

⁂ The widow whose loss of her husband of many decades feels like abrupt withdrawal of all the joy life has to offer and a sentence to despair.

⁂ The gangly, awkward teenager (with changing voice) no one ever wants on the football, baseball, or soccer team.

⁂ The young man, emaciated from AIDS and with purple splotches on his face, who knows he will not live to celebrate another Christmas or birthday.

⁂ The divorced woman who has been rejected by her ex-husband's family and is trying to cope with raising four children alone.

⁂ The elderly woman with heart failure living alone on a low income whose friends are gone, who has no children, and who feels no one has time for her any more.

✿ The painfully shy, stuttering student who can't answer a teacher's question in class without a chorus of laughter from her classmates.

✿ The homeless, physically abused old man with a deep cough and a limp who doubts he will survive another year on the streets.

✿ The pregnant, unmarried fifteen-year-old who has told no one of her pregnancy and fears her parents would order her to leave the house if they knew.

When the Old Testament prophet Isaiah promised the people of Israel a savior, he prophesied that a suffering servant would come, one who knows what it is to feel our pain. The vulnerable infant born in a stable was not to be a powerful David, a kingly figure who would redeem Israel by His physical might. This would be a very human savior, one who would Himself undergo rejection and feel despised for our sake: "He was despised and rejected by men; / a man of sorrows, and acquainted with grief; / and as one from whom men hide their faces / he was despised, and we esteemed him not" (Isaiah 53:3).

Jesus' gift of God's unconditional acceptance is all the more precious because it was bought at such a costly price. As Isaiah puts it, "But he was wounded for our transgressions, / he was bruised for our iniquities; / upon him was the chastisement that made us whole, / and with his stripes we are healed. / All we like sheep have gone astray; / we have turned every one to his own way; / and the LORD has laid on him / the iniquity of us all" (53:5-6).

Betrayed by His closest friends, left to die a brutal death on the cross — a death reserved for the basest of criminals — Jesus can comfort us and enfold us to Himself with complete understanding of our suffering. He understands because He Himself has felt what we feel.

And so the child Jesus, the innocent human and divine infant sent to bring us enduring, unconditional love, holds out His arms to us in countless nativity scenes during the Christmas season. Jesus' arms issue an open invitation: *Lay down your burdens of rejection, abandonment, loneliness, and despair. I want you. I will love you as no other can. Come to Me.*

Please Don't Touch

Walking toward Capitol Hill from Union Station in the warming air of a sunny pre-springtime day, I stopped in a little park not far from two massive U.S. Senate buildings to notice the daffodils poking their heads up for some sunshine. Near them, a squirrel stretched his elongated body out on the scaly bark of a tree trunk head down and bushy tail up, spreading his legs and getting a purchase on the bark with his sharp claws.

I'll just pause awhile before the Senate hearing, I thought, heading for the park bench I saw just ahead. But — something was different about this park bench. I stood looking at it, my mouth open in astonishment. I hardly heard the squirrel as he scurried down the tree and went off into the bushes to dig for a buried nut.

The park bench was wooden and had black wrought-iron arms on both ends like others I'd seen, but this one also had two extra black wrought-iron arms on the central part of the bench itself, so that three people could sit there separated from one another by the partitions of the extra arms. Three people could sit there and look straight ahead, not at one another, and never touch elbows. I had never seen a park bench like this one before. There was something forbidding and punitive about it, as if it belonged in the yard of a strictly run school, jail, or mental hospital. *(Sit right there and don't move until I tell you to, all three of you.)*

Here, in the shadow of the legislators who trod the marble halls of the capital of the United States, someone — but probably not someone as important as a congressman — had decreed that benches in this park should have partitions to separate human beings. Why?

The signal this bench sent was unmistakable: Please don't touch. *If I sit down next to you, look straight ahead, and pretend you don't see me; I'll do the same, and we can pretend we don't even know the other one is there.*

Who had deemed such partitions necessary? What was their real message? That strangers must never, ever brush up against one another, not even so much as the cloth of their jacketed arms? That a homeless person who bathed infrequently might want to sit next to a freshly showered legislative staff person and thus had to be kept within the confines of his own seat? That human beings must have their own space to maintain their privacy, especially in public places?

What if two friends came here and sat down next to each other, talking, and then a third person, a stranger, came by to sit down and eat his lunch? Would the two who were talking look sideways at the one who was eating, wishing he wouldn't chew or crumple his napkin so loudly? Would they, in fact, wish he hadn't come at all, or even get up and leave, looking for another bench where they could be together and talk with no interruption? What if three friends came here and sat down; what kind of hierarchy would they honor, and whom would they place in the middle? What if three strangers came? Would they speak? Would one hold the half-outspread newspaper to his chest tightly, his face hidden behind it, hoping he wouldn't be interrupted while he read?

Whoever had put the extra arms on these park benches was clever. It was a little thing, really, just a few extra dollars for some metal grillwork and some screws and a workman's time; it wouldn't cost the taxpayers much extra money. The wrought-iron partitions looked new; they must not have been here very long.

But there was a problem. I saw other park benches with similar partitions in this little triangle of green, and no one was sitting on them. Not a single soul on this sunny pre-springtime day with daffodils budding and birds chortling in the high bare branches that reached up to the sky like arms wanting sunshine was sitting on a single partitioned park bench. Across the street from the park, in front of Union Station, where trains pulled in and out all day long, stood two tall flagpoles flying the American flag. Not a single person was sitting on one of these park benches to admire how the flags of the free caught the breeze that still had a bit of the briskness of winter about it.

More than one person in this normally busy little park between Union Station and the two Senate office buildings had gotten the message, but it wasn't the one whoever had thought of the extra partitions on the park benches had intended. The message the passersby had apparently gotten was one that said, *I won't sit here; I don't like this bench.* Maybe they had even thought, *Why do we need partitions between us on park benches? Aren't there enough divisions between us already?*

Once when Jesus was standing among a crowd preaching in parables and telling of the gospel of forgiveness for those who accepted the Holy Spirit, His mother and His brothers came and, standing outside the crowd, sent for Him. The crowd was sitting around Him, completely surrounding Him, and some among them said, "Your mother and your brothers are outside, asking for you." But Jesus replied, "Who are my mother and my brothers?" And, looking at the faces of those who sat around Him, he said, "Here are my mother and my brothers! Whoever does the will of God is my brother, and sister, and mother." (See Matthew 12:46-50, Mark 3:31-35, and Luke 8:19-21.)

Is it really possible to partition our lives, as someone had partitioned these park benches? Can we partition our affections, our concerns for others? Are some people more worthy of sitting next to than others? Isn't the Christian message about getting rid of partitions, wherever we find them? For, as Paul tells us, we are neither Jew nor Greek, but sisters and brothers in Christ. We do not need partitions on park benches, and we do not need them in our hearts. Jesus, the revolutionary for love, spent His short life breaking barriers down, barriers between the poor and the wealthy, the sinner and the scribe, the sick and the well. Shouldn't we try to do the same?

Now, as I stood by this partitioned park bench and ran my hand over the cold wrought iron, I felt the chill in this pre-springtime air more keenly, and I turned up the collar of my black raincoat. But this time I couldn't tell if the chill came from the March breeze or from the sight and feel of these wrought-iron barriers, partitions someone had thought to put here to keep human beings apart.

Father Martin's Reclamation

The thirty-four-year-old man knelt in the chapel. His brilliant blue eyes were lowered; his red hair shone in the dim light. His Irish humor made him a popular teacher among the seminary students at St. Charles College in Catonsville, Maryland. But, at this solemn moment, he felt consumed by shame. He was, he had to admit, addicted to alcohol.

God, he prayed, *drinking threatens my priesthood and my life. I've tried and tried to stop, but I keep failing. I know your grace is available to me. I believe you will show me the instrument of your healing. Amen.*

For ten years, Father Joseph C. Martin had struggled and prayed to overcome his addiction and to receive God's healing. There were trips to the hospital and brief periods of sobriety. But his craving for alcohol continued.

Finally, in June 1958, shortly after his visit to the chapel, his superiors in the Roman Catholic Church sent him to Guest House, a treatment center for alcoholics, in Lake Orion, Michigan. On his arrival there, Father Martin stood before Austin Ripley, a recovering alcoholic who had created Guest House to provide priests with their own Alcoholics Anonymous (AA) program.

"Our philosophy is to treat every sick priest as if he were Christ Himself," Ripley told him. "If you want sobriety, it is available, with God's help. You are here to get well. And you *will* get well, if you believe you can."

For the first time since his ordination in 1948, Father Martin felt that God was directing him — this time, to a way out of his private hell. The man God chose to show him that way was Dr. Walter Green, the center's medical director. As Dr. Green explained to him that alcoholism is a chemical addiction, not a moral failure, Father Martin instantly felt his burden being lifted. He learned that his previous attempts to stop drinking had failed because he was powerless over a physiological disease he did not understand.

During the dark years of his struggle with alcohol, Father Martin had never ceased praying, had never given up his faith that God would help him overcome his problem. Now, he realized that God, through Guest House, was giving him the tools to overcome his chemical addiction. And he set his mind on sobriety.

Applying the principles of AA, Father Martin admitted, "I'm an alcoholic, and it is *my* problem." He learned to use the love and fellowship surrounding him to nurture and reinforce his own desire to stop drinking. He began to think of positive ways he could reconstruct his life on the basis of sobriety. He did this daily, by accepting the AA way, which says, "Don't drink today, and maybe — probably — things will be a bit better tomorrow."

He also learned to let each day of sobriety be a small success, so that one success could build on another. He examined his life in depth, recognizing the bad, but focusing on the good. As he began experiencing the joys of sobriety, he concentrated on the gifts he could use for God.

In January 1959, fortified by the lessons of Guest House, Father Martin returned to St. Charles College. He was determined to remain sober. Wanting to turn his painful experience into a positive influence on others, he began talking to local groups about alcoholism. His message was simple: Alcoholism is a disease; the alcoholic is not immoral, but sick. The alcoholic has a terminal illness that must be treated. The alcoholic cannot get well alone, but needs help to attain sobriety. Most important, the alcoholic is a person of value who needs care and love.

In 1969, as the number of young men entering the priesthood shrank, Father Martin's teaching job was phased out. He was offered a post as an educator with the state of Maryland's Division of Alcoholism Control. With the permission of Church authorities, he accepted it. Two years later, he made a film, *Chalk Talk on Alcohol*, for the U.S. Navy. It was so popular — and effective — that it catapulted Father Martin into the national spotlight. The film became the principal educational vehicle on alcoholism for most branches of the federal government, especially the Armed Services, and is used widely by companies, medical facilities, and rehabilitation programs.

Besieged with speaking requests from around the world, Father Martin, with the blessing of his bishop, became a full-time lecturer and educator on alcoholism. He was now convinced that God had called him to help people struggling with addiction.

In 1978, Father Martin was flying home from South Carolina with Mae Abraham, a recovering alcoholic who, with her husband, Tommy, had befriended the priest.

"You know, Father," Mrs. Abraham said over the hum of the engines, "you could talk about alcoholism until you die. Why don't we build a place where everything you stand for can go on after you?"

Father Martin reflected on his friend's suggestion: *The cross on which Christ died was, in His time, a symbol of shame; thieves were crucified on it. But Christ embraced the cross and turned it into the symbol of Christianity. My cross is alcoholism. By embracing it as a gift from God, I can touch people the way others can't, and give them the gift of healing I have received.*

Father Martin remembered something Austin Ripley had told him at Guest House, something he hadn't understood at the time: "You will be able to do what popes cannot." In that moment, the vision of what he could give others became clear. He could use his struggle for sobriety as proof to others that God will help them overcome any adversity.

Over a period of months, Father Martin formed a plan for a tax-exempt, nonprofit treatment center for alcoholics. What followed, however, were years of hard work, false starts, and disappointments. A site was found and then, because of the high cost of building, was lost. A beautiful estate was purchased, but renovation costs escalated. The struggle to raise funds went on for five years. But Father Martin never gave up. Instead, he held on to his dream, and that dream gave him the strength and perseverance to continue. Finally, Ashley — named in honor of Mae Abraham's parents — opened on January 17, 1983.

Today, Ashley's three impeccably decorated buildings on a beautiful site along the Chesapeake Bay in Havre de Grace, Maryland, resemble a fine resort. Its forty-three-acre complex of grounds, chapel, and restful rooms in a Stanford White mansion — even its tail-wagging resident yellow Labrador — says to each addict, "You are a person of worth; have hope." A recovering alcoholic who is a member of Ashley's board says, "When you walk in the door, you feel you've come home."

Coming home to a loving, nonjudgmental family is the

heart of Father Martin's basic thirty-day program. Residents, usually sixty at a time, attend lectures, listen to tapes, watch films, and participate in personal counseling and small-group therapy sessions. To leaven the often-draining programs, residents are encouraged to engage in team sports, attend cookouts, take trips, or to spend quiet time walking or fishing. Permeating each activity at Ashley is Christ's message of unconditional love for each human being. Father Martin celebrates Mass every day, and spiritual counseling is available for those who seek it.

The principles of AA guide Ashley's staff members, numbering more than a hundred. All of the counselors are themselves recovering alcoholics. They view their mission as showing Ashley residents support that says, "You, too, can do it." As Father Martin puts it, "We say, 'Here's the door, come on through.' "

Many alcoholics are tortured by the harm they have inflicted on others. Father Martin tries to share his forward-looking vision, his belief that anything can be forgiven. He tells them that they must set aside all the baggage of the past and begin a new life. "The past is forgiven," he tells them. "No matter what your life was like, it was only bad if you don't learn from it and build on it." Most Ashley graduates — who number more than ten thousand — begin new lives of sobriety. The recovery rate of Ashley alumni is more than seventy percent. Ashley is recognized by health-care providers as one of America's most successful programs for the treatment of alcoholism and chemical addiction. It is especially well known for its relapse prevention program and its emphasis on involving family members in the treatment. Ashley graduates include government officials, homemakers, students, and business executives.

One who is glad he came through the Ashley door is Michael K. Deaver, a White House aide during Ronald Reagan's presidency. It was Father Martin's positive spiritual force, Deaver says, that brought him out of the despair that alcohol caused. "Father Martin's affirmative attitude permeates Ashley," says Deaver, now a public-relations executive and a member of Ashley's board.

At a graduation ceremony in May, the joy of newfound sobriety fills one of Ashley's fieldstone halls. Father Martin stands at the podium. His hair is white; his figure, portly. But his eyes are the same clear blue, and his voice remains deep and strong. "There won't be even a five-second excerpt of this event on the evening news," he tells the assembled graduates. "But, of all your graduations, none compares with this one. Today, each of you is your own valedictorian. If you want sobriety, it is available. You have been touched by the hand of God; it is absolutely impossible to be touched by the hand of God and remain the same."

Father Martin then holds up a gold-colored medal. "We present each of you with the Ashley medallion. We didn't pay much for it. But you paid — with your pain, and with the pain your disease inflicted on those you love. There is no price tag on this medallion."

One by one, the graduates walk up to the podium. A classically pretty, well-groomed woman in her late twenties says, "I learned a lot about myself here: how to keep a positive attitude and be a winner." Years of going into treatment programs and quitting had preceded her trip to Ashley. Tears fill her eyes as she recalls the unconditional love she has been shown here.

Next, a man in his early thirties stands at the podium, looks out over the audience, and says: "At Ashley, I began to understand, for the first time, something my grandfather always says: 'Any morning you wake up and can put your feet on the ground is a good day.' Here, I learned to look at my life in a new way and see that I have things to offer. I've never seen a more loving community anywhere. I thank all of you for allowing me to see myself through you."

Another man in his mid-thirties struggles with tears. "I spent years getting here," he says. "Powerless and unmanageable — that was me. Now, I've come to respect that priceless part of me that is in all of us. And I've learned that love is the only drug that works." On the word love, his voice breaks and he has to struggle to finish. When he does, everyone claps, none harder than Father Martin, who has not taken a drink of alcohol in more than four decades.

As he watched the smiling faces of his new graduates, Father Joseph C. Martin thought about the long road he has traveled from his own private hell to Ashley. On that journey, he has not only received God's healing miracle in controlling his own addiction, but he has become God's tool for working healing miracles in the lives of others. He has transformed his private pain into joy — for himself and for thousands of others.

Saving Throwaway Children

They walk the streets of any major city, these hungry-faced children with old eyes and nowhere to belong.

That freckle-faced thirteen-year-old boy in the torn jeans could be your son. He has no mother to put iron-on patches on his jeans. That fifteen-year-old girl with heavy mascara and a long curly black braid could be your daughter. She has no father to care whether she's done her homework for tomorrow.

The freckle-faced boy and the girl with the curly braid are today's throwaway children. For whatever reason, they have left whatever homes they had, these wandering children, and have chosen to confront a hostile world that's too big, too harsh, too greedy. Too late, usually, these children with old eyes learn that the world will use them up and toss them aside when their bodies are no longer healthy or supple. In a free country where a child's sexual favors can be bought for less than the price of a restaurant dinner, youth and health are essential; sickness isn't in style. Too late, these children will be victimized by pimps or pushers, or succumb to AIDS or a drug overdose.

Does anybody out there care? Someone cares, and she is a soft-pillow-looking kind of person (with a tough fibrous core) called Sister Mary Rose McGeady. If you were a child in pain, she'd be the kind of surrogate grandmother you'd look for, when you could bring yourself to ask an adult for help.

Sister Mary Rose is president of Covenant House, the largest crisis center and shelter for runaway children in the country. Covenant House started in New York City and has now expanded into Atlantic City and Newark, New Jersey; Fort Lauderdale, Florida; New Orleans, Louisiana; Hollywood, California; Houston, Texas; Anchorage, Alaska; Washington, D.C.; Detroit, Michigan; and Orlando, Florida. Sister Mary Rose has opened additional Covenant Houses in Toronto and Vancouver, Canada, as well as in Guatemala, Mexico, Honduras, and Nicaragua. New Covenant Houses are planned for Philadelphia, Pennsylvania; St. Louis, Missouri; and Oakland, California.

What worries Sister Mary Rose, who has celebrated fifty

years as a Daughter of Charity, is time: not having enough of it to do what she knows needs to be done. "I've never been afraid of dying. But I worry about running out of time," is how she puts it. Time is important to her because with the ticking of the clock and the passing of the hours and days and months and years come new children, thousands of new children, who are hurting and have been abused by adults. "Covenant House has, in essence, become a massive sanctuary for America's youngest and most lost hearts and souls," is how this nun sees her mission. And she knows that mission must go on into a future of children's pain and despair even as she herself cannot.

She tells of Nancy, who was so overwhelmed with self-loathing that she covered her entire head with a red hood, never taking it off for weeks at a time. She tells of Liz, who thinks of herself as nothing but a "mule," a girl whose identity lay in swallowing cocaine stuffed in little plastic bags and thus smuggling it inside her person. She tells of David, whose stepfather beat him and got into bed with him and made him do things David knows are ugly and perverted.

Sister Mary Rose knows that she, personally, is running out of time for all the Nancys and Lizzes and Davids that will keep coming to Covenant House, one way or another — furtively calling the shelter's hotline from a phone booth, or showing up at the door because someone, another girl or boy on the street, said to go there when you didn't have anywhere else to go. And she knows something else, something that brings a different, more cutting kind of pain to her heart.

In recent years, Covenant House has been serving the needs of a different kind of child: a throwaway child, not a runaway child. These throwaway children are generally the oldest in a family, and when they reach a certain age — maybe eighteen, maybe seventeen, maybe sixteen — their parents show them the door, telling them it's time to go out and make their own way, earn a living somehow. Sometimes the parents say, "I did it at your age, so can you." These older children become too expensive to feed and clothe, it seems, or their adolescent mood swings become too difficult to address (there are younger children in the house, after all). And so out they go: unskilled, hungry, not much in the way of job prospects, easy prey for street prowlers. Sister Mary Rose wants them. She'll take in these throwaway children and try to restore to them some sense that they're worth something.

Not everyone can be a Sister Mary Rose McGeady. The work is hard, long, discouraging, and dangerous — especially when you tangle with pimps. Even a nun's habit is little protection against some of the master exploiters whose livelihood depends on child prostitution. Not everyone can communicate with street children the way Sister Mary Rose can, nor gather them around her comfortably, breaking through the walls of their tight little faces. Not everyone can walk the Minnesota Strip — a fifteen-block stretch of Manhattan's Eighth Avenue — where drifters, prostitutes, pimps, and runaway children scratch a living out of ravenous sexual hunger and twisted needs.

Sister Mary Rose's feet have ached; her soul has ached.

No, we're not all Sister Mary Roses, nor were we meant to be. But we can do what we can to help. We can reach out to our young people, we can listen to them, and we can love them. We can, sometimes, prevent their turning to the street by convincing them to stay at home. We can, sometimes, keep them from taking the first step toward prostitution or drug addiction. And we can refuse to support the sex-for-sale industry that enslaves the bodies of young runaways.

Here are some nonjudgmental guidelines we can all follow to help our children:

※ We can reach out to hurting children — our own, a friend of our own child, a grandchild, a neighbor's teenager, a member of a youth group. We can show such children by our actions, sometimes just stopping to talk for a while, that we care what happens to them.

※ We can use our voices to say, "Children cannot and must not be bought and sold." Each child is precious to us and to God. We can speak out publicly against child exploitation and prostitution.

※ We can use our feet and our wallets to boycott any establishment that sells pornographic literature or rents out hard-core porn videos.

※ We can live by moral and ethical principles that teach children, by example, the values we want them to have.

※ We can teach our children about sex and family and marriage, telling them what we want them to hear, not what they will hear from actors in a television sitcom. We can ask our churches to help us in youth groups and Bible study for children.

※ We can urge our pastors to do more for young people, not only through Bible study but also through youth retreats and discussion groups on social issues that confuse and frighten. How else will a scared child be able to learn about AIDS or drug abuse or pedophilia in a loving, supportive Christian context?

※ We can publicize the Covenant House Nineline, a toll-free, twenty-four-hour help line for children and worried parents of troubled children. The number is 1-800-999-9999.

Like Sister Mary Rose of Covenant House, St. Francis of Assisi was worried about time. At the end of his life, St. Francis left one request with his friends: "Brothers and Sisters, while we have time, let us do good."

Combating Racial Hatred

Harold P. Freeman, M.D., is a scholarly, quiet-voiced black doctor who lived half his life as an American under legalized segregation. When he is not wearing a white lab coat or surgical scrubs, he dresses in the dark, conservatively tailored suits medical professionals favor.

Harold Freeman neither looks nor talks nor acts like a man who would disrupt the establishment. After all, he *is* the establishment: He is director of surgery at Harlem Hospital Center and chairman of the President's Cancer Panel. Freeman is sought after as a speaker and writer; he is constantly invited to medical conferences and put on panels.

But make no mistake: Freeman makes waves of the highest, most well-placed order when it comes to combating racism in America. Freeman made waves when he stated that an American male in New York City's Harlem has a lower life expectancy than a male in Bangladesh — one of the poorest countries of the world. Freeman made more waves when the President's Cancer Panel he heads released a daring report — with his name prominently at the top — stating that the concept of race has no scientific basis in fact.

The panel's report states that scientists now estimate that "all externally visible traits represent only 0.01% expression of each individual's 100,000 genes." These superficial visible traits are inherited individually, and are not transmitted in genetic clusters. The bottom line is that there are no "black genes." There are no "Asian genes." There are families who may have a specific gene or gene mutation (change), but these are not due to "race genes." Moreover, America is becoming a multiracial culture. It is estimated that between three fourths and nine tenths of African Americans have some white ancestry, and about one fourth have Native American ancestry. In other words, we are all far more alike than we are different.

Freeman's panel found that despite this lack of scientific evidence for racial distinctions, racism permeates all levels of U.S. society — including science. But it may be so subtle that it is "transparent to those in the dominant population group." The message is that we may discriminate against those of another race without even realizing it.

In a country that finds itself increasingly splintered into ethnic groups — African Americans, Hispanic Americans, Asian Americans — it is easy to stick together comfortably in groups where everyone is "like us." Too easy. It is also too easy to do nothing when confronted with hatred based on racial or ethnic differences.

We're all too aware that the road Jesus wants us to take isn't the easy or comfortable one. Rioting in the nation's inner cities (New York and Los Angeles, for instance) has focused painful attention on the fact that the Christian ideal of valuing each human being's priceless worth — no matter what his skin color or ethnic origins — is far from a national reality and requires constant effort to achieve.

The example Christ gave us was one of ultimate tolerance, forgiveness, and acceptance. Totally without class consciousness, He accepted and loved all human beings, no matter who they were or what they had done. He ate with publicans and sinners, and when the Pharisees rebuked His actions, He replied, "I came not to call the righteous, but sinners" (Matthew 9:13). Jesus refused to pass judgment on Mary when she sat at His feet to hear His words and neglected dinner preparations, despite the anger of her sister, Martha; instead He gently chided Martha for criticizing her sister for wanting to hear God's word (see Luke 10:38-42).

Jesus did not die for an elite few, but for all — tax collectors, murderers, prostitutes. Even in His agony on the cross, He could look past His suffering to comfort the convicted criminal hanging next to Him by saying, "Truly, I say to you, today you will be with me in Paradise" (Luke 23:43). If we really try hard to follow this example, we will strive to be loving peacemakers in all of our dealings with others.

Current evidence indicates that the world desperately needs more loving peacemakers. A public television program on hatred narrated by journalist Bill Moyers made the point that hatred against others who are different is a kind of glue that holds ethnic groups together. The "us against them" mind-set leads to the dehumanizing of entire racial groups, a dehumanization that says it's all right to steal, pillage, or even kill because the victimizer does not view his victim as a person of value. Those who live by hatred are energized by their inner poison and feel powerful only when they are destroying a person or group with whom they feel no link or unity.

As human beings, we would like to think we have learned the lesson of Adolf Hitler's Nazi Germany well. Hitler, thoroughly convinced that his personal racial hatred was for the benefit of all mankind, was able to regard an entire racial group as subhuman and worthy of extermination. Surely such racial hatred could not flourish today — or could it? In fact, it does, as documented in a chilling article in an issue of *Jewish Monthly* on the rising right in modern Germany.

In that article, Nazi propaganda, regalia, demonstrations, and tee shirts are portrayed as all the vogue in eastern Berlin among youths who believe in white supremacy. As one of these neo-Nazis articulated: "As I am white, I must work for the white race. We must close the doors of Europe and make Germany free of foreigners." The word "foreigners," of course, is used to designate anyone different. The tee shirts are not just harmless mementos of a forgotten era; one, for example, proclaims "no remorse" above a picture of Hitler with a swastika behind him. Below the picture are the words "One day the world will know . . . Adolf Hitler was right!"

How can we respond in a constructive way to hatred in our own lives? How can we be the instruments of love Jesus is calling us to be? We can start in small but important ways, such as:

* Speaking up against bigotry and racial prejudice calmly but firmly when they come up in conversations with others.

* Making an effort to befriend people in our own church who are of a different ethnic group.

* Celebrating cultural diversity by holding ethnic food festivals and craft fairs in our neighborhoods.

* Inviting people from different ethnic backgrounds to speak about the countries of their parentage at church meetings.

* Inviting people from different cultural heritages to come to small-group meetings as guests.

* Making a point of patronizing minority-owned businesses such as restaurants and bakeries and getting to know their owners by becoming regular customers.

* Reading about other cultures in magazines, newspapers, and books.

❀ Seeking volunteer opportunities to work with children or adults from other cultures, such as English literacy programs.

Those who practice hatred may be misguided, but they believe they have good reasons for doing so. Similarly, those who practice love must also believe they have good reasons for being instruments of peace. In a world where good and evil remain locked in a combat zone, crimes of hate can only be countered by acts of love.

In his letter to the president, the one accompanying the President's Cancer Panel report on race, Harold Freeman said, "Science can be a crucial element in the Nation's most important mission of building one America."

So can love.

Who Is the Giver?

She is known as "Dr. Sister" in tiny Tutwiler, Mississippi, where she runs the Tutwiler Clinic for poor, mostly black residents in the little towns of the area. Sister Anne Brooks, both a nun and a doctor of osteopathy, binds up wounds, diagnoses cancer, battles children's skin sores from impetigo, holds the hands of the dying, and prescribes drugs to treat high blood pressure and relieve the pain of arthritis.

It is hard work, being a healer in a town where there is little money to pay for the high-tech medicine found in large urban centers. The payments of the clinic's patients cover less than one fourth of the expenses of the clinic. Every month, Sister Anne sends out fifty to seventy letters to drug companies, pleading to get free drugs on a compassionate basis for her indigent patients. The pharmaceutical company forms for free drugs for the poor keep changing; the paperwork is enough to discourage the most dedicated physician.

The Tutwiler Clinic patients' money problems are worse since the U.S. welfare program effectively ended, to be replaced by temporary assistance. Tutwiler is located in Tallahatchie County in the traditionally agricultural area of the Mississippi Delta, where deteriorating economic conditions have pressed on the people like a mean Southern wind. Making ends meet is hard when you live on less than $10,000 a year, especially when there is a rule that people can have food stamps for only three months of the year. What about the other nine?

Work is catch-as-catch-can, if you can. The picture-frame factory and the sewing factory — both a source of jobs — have closed. Casinos, which pay well, are offering jobs — but Tutwiler residents have to commute a total of six hours by bus to and from the casinos, which are near Memphis. There are jobs at the chicken factories and the fish factories, but getting there also involves long commutes. Tutwiler residents work when they can. They pay the clinic what they can, when they can. Private donations and grants make up the rest. Sister Anne's minimal living expenses are paid by her order, the Sisters of the Holy Names of Jesus and Mary.

Day care centers don't open at 4:00 A.M., when some residents have to leave for their long commutes to work. Thus families are stressed, and abuse of all kinds is common. Grandmothers end up taking care of young children, while many of the grandmothers have health problems that send them to the Tutwiler Clinic and are long past the age when they can run after toddlers. The grandmothers try, but their love for the children is tested every day. "Through all of this muck the women stand strong," said Sister Anne. "In spite of it all, the folks keep on keeping on."

The hours are long and the medical problems are often severe: malnutrition in skinny children and wizened elderly people with no money for nourishing food; permanently bent backs from osteoarthritis caused by picking cotton. It's discouraging not being able to write prescriptions for the medicines the people need or order medical tests without having to worry about money. It's disheartening to see medical problems that could have been prevented if the patient had had the money to pay for treatment years earlier.

Sister Anne — a soft-spoken middle-aged woman with closely cropped hair and twinkling eyes behind her glasses — could have left Tutwiler in July 1987 when her four-year obligation to the National Health Service Corps, which paid for her medical training, ended. She could have gone someplace where the poorest of the poor and the lack of education are not so much in evidence, and where the medical problems are less intractable.

But Sister Anne chose to stay in Tallahatchie County in little Tutwiler. Why?

The easy answer would be to say that the people's needs were so great she felt she couldn't leave. But that's not it.

When she was honored for service to others in Washington, D.C., by the America's Awards programs, a project of the late Norman Vincent Peale, Sister Anne looked out over an auditorium of thousands and said exactly why she stayed. She stayed, she said, because the people gave her far more than she could ever give them. She said she felt a bond with the people, a link that went far beyond the doctor-patient relationship.

She told of going to see a young man to tell him he had terminal cancer and of breaking into tears. Instead of reacting with self-absorbed fear or anger (which would have been natural for someone acutely ill), the young man told the Sister-doctor not to worry or feel sad; *he* comforted *her*. He gave her a gift of compassion because he was able to think of her, not of himself.

Then there was the hospitalized patient who was just about to go to surgery. Sister Anne stopped by to ask the woman how she was doing. "The Lord is my shepherd," the woman replied in a voice full of confidence and faith. There wasn't much to say that could top that, so "I simply had to join in and the two of us continued through the whole Psalm together," said Sister Anne.

People like the young man with cancer and the woman about to have surgery are Sister Anne's family. She can't leave her family. "When the takeover of a company results in no supplies or technical support for our lab machine; and our eight-ton furnace gives up the ghost after thirty-four years of life; and a company that makes heart medicine deems a very ill sixty-two-year-old cardiac patient unqualified for their product (although he cannot work and therefore has no income) — what else is there to do but echo that Psalm of faith and trust?" she said.

So at the Tutwiler Clinic in Tallahatchie County, Mississippi, Sister Anne keeps on keeping on and, as she pointed out, "The Lord keeps on looking after us." She is mindful of the Bible story of the poor widow of Zarephath who made bread for the prophet Elijah from the last of the flour she needed for herself and her son to live on. Because she helped Elijah from her meager supply, the widow was richly rewarded with oil and flour that didn't run out (see 1 Kings 17:8-16).

Due to a generous grant from a private foundation, Tutwiler patients receive weekly dental care from a dentist and are able to see an eye doctor once a month. The eye doctor's visits are a special gift to diabetics, whose disease can cause blindness. Private donations surged after the television program *60 Minutes* did a segment on Sister Anne in 1990 and aired it again in 1991 (but donations have dropped to half since then).

Because of one especially generous grant, Tutwiler now has a brand new Community Education Center, a tiled-floor center so beautiful that one elderly woman came and sat in the wide hall under the light from the skylight just to have her spirit nourished. "I truly think the center is where health begins," said Sister Anne. At a health fair held there, people received testing for blood pressure, blood cholesterol levels, and blood sugar. Printed handouts on diet, exercise, and health lifestyles were passed out, along with gifts of caps, tee shirts, and soap. The refreshments were healthy snacks that tasted good and were good for the body.

In the Community Education Center there is a computer library; there are play programs for children aged two to four; classes to help residents work toward a high school equivalency degree; a homework club where teenagers (who are paid the minimum wage) help younger children do their schoolwork; and classes in self-respect and effective parenting. The community center can be rented for wedding receptions and funerals. The community center is a place of children's laughter, of learning, and of joy. But Sister Anne is already looking ahead. "Our big dream is to put up a gym," she said. There should be a gym because there ought to be someplace safe for the young men to gather, someplace where they can shoot baskets in Tutwiler and maybe dream of shooting baskets on a college campus.

There is a lot more to do in Tutwiler, and it requires a lot of giving. But somehow that keeping-on spirit of the people transforms difficult, emotionally grinding work into a gift that comes straight back to the giver. What is often forgotten in discussions about work with the poor, the homeless, the hungry, and the sick is the gifts these "least of the least" of God's people can and do give to the giver.

Sister Anne knows that a mind-set that separates "us" from "them" dehumanizes both giver and recipient by setting up a barrier between them and by emphasizing the differences between the poor and those who serve them. Far more important than those differences of circumstance are the shared human bonds that make us one in God's community. Those bonds are the wellspring of compassion, empathy, and love. Those bonds make giving to others a privilege, not a chore. Those bonds unite all of us by nourishing the spirit. Those bonds are the reason a poor young man dying of cancer can think of his doctor's feelings, not his own, and the reason a woman about to go to surgery can reassure her doctor by quoting the Twenty-third Psalm in a strong, sure voice.

Those bonds have nothing to do with pocketbook or social status.

And so when people like Sister Anne Brooks receive awards, it is not surprising that they focus not on the award but on the gifts the people they serve give to them. They are not just being noble; they are being honest.

Who is really the giver here?

Standing Up to a Culture of Violence

She was the kind of quietly pretty, sweet girl you'd like to invite to dinner. Mary Anne had black hair, hazel eyes, fair skin, and an open expression that was somewhere between questioning and a smile. Hers was a trusting face, and it was vulnerable.

When I worked with Mary Anne — which I did for several years — she never raised her voice, never criticized anyone in the office, never seemed overwhelmed by stress, never refused to do a task. She seemed far above office gossip and willing to shoulder more than her load, a rarity in any profession. I liked her a lot. I also liked the fact that Mary Anne was upfront about her faith; she was a devout Catholic who very clearly incorporated a nonjudgmental, peaceful approach to life into her work.

When I got the news about Mary Anne by telephone, I had to ask to have it repeated. "What?" I asked. "What?" It wasn't that I hadn't heard, it was that I couldn't process what I was hearing from the other end of the telephone receiver: Mary Anne had been murdered. I wanted to throw the phone down in denial, or — better yet — call her immediately and hear her say in her soft voice that it wasn't true, that it couldn't be true because she was talking to me, right now.

The facts, as they came out, were brutally spare and simple: Mary Anne had been tied up, gagged, and bludgeoned to death in a basement in Baltimore, Maryland, by a disturbed young man she had known for years, but had not seen for a while. It came out in the stories that it was Mary Anne's trusting nature that led to her death; had she not seen the best in the disturbed young man, she would never have gone into a house with him.

I had not worked with Mary Anne for several years, but I found myself thinking of her obsessively. What did she do and think when he tied her up? Did she fight to escape? (I could not imagine gentle Mary Anne using physical force.) Did she plead with him? Did she pray, calling on the name of her Savior or His mother to deliver her from what she could now see was an evil beyond her ability to turn into good? Did she cry? Did she think of her mother and father, and how she wished she could see them one more time? Did she think of how this incident would change their lives if it ended hers? Did she wish she could have spared them that pain (for that would have been like her)?

Mary Anne, whose dark, gentle Italian-American good looks would doubtless have attracted the right kind of husband, now would never put on a white dress and veil and walk down a church aisle to marry, never have a child, never see another sunset, never sniff another rose, never eat another ice-cream cone. For months, tears of outrage and regret for Mary Anne and all she would miss ran down my cheeks every time I thought of her.

Like the lives of many Americans, mine had been suddenly touched by the brutality of a violent culture. Mary Anne — my friend and former colleague at work — was dead by another's hand. Mary Anne, her family, the husband she would never have and all of us who knew her, had been victimized.

Followers of Christ are taught from the cradle to turn the other cheek and always to respect the rights of another human soul. After all, that soul is precious in the sight of God. By that credo I must forgive and pray for Mary Anne's assailant. I find it hard, but I am trying.

My dilemma isn't unusual. How, exactly, are Christians to put their beliefs about forgiveness and the sacredness of life to work in a culture that thrives on violence as vultures thrive on the dead meat of road kill?

I live just outside Washington, D.C., a city that has been called "the murder capital of the nation." My house has been robbed twice — once by drug addicts who left profane messages on my tape recorder — and I have had my purse snatched. The mail truck in my neighborhood was robbed — despite stiff federal penalties for stealing mail. I have no way of knowing what I might be missing in that mail delivery.

I have known people who were brutally assaulted, people whose cars have been stolen, and people whose homes were broken into. I have known women who were raped.

Violence affects us all, no matter how hard we try to ignore it and to insulate ourselves from it. In the United States, violence is so pervasive that it seems woven into the very fabric of daily life. Consider these multifaceted forms of violence:

* Murder for money or drugs.

* Rape or assault as a means of relieving pent-up aggression.

* Stealing someone else's property.

* Sexual exploitation of the bodies of women and children in pornographic acts and suggestive ads so as to make money.

* Attempts to destroy the family by blatant temptation — some by supposedly well-meaning "friends" — to indulge in alcohol abuse, adultery, recreational drugs, or easy divorce.

* Visual assaults by films and television that subject viewers to gratuitous gore and dismemberment.

* Assault on the ears by modern music, as in the use of repetitive, amplified lyrics to sell subliminal messages honoring the black arts of satanic cults.

* Psychological abuse, as in screaming foul words at a child and undermining his self-esteem.

* Abuse of the land, as in littering it with trash or hazardous wastes.

The list above is short; there are many more items that could be added. Faced with this onslaught against our senses and sensibilities, we have two choices: either to go along with the mainstream flow of modern culture or to say, "I can't live with this."

The choice is clear: We can't and shouldn't accept what we see and hear all around us. Part of our role as witnesses to Christ's word is to stand up and bring the hope of harmony and healing to an increasingly sick world. Instead of despairing, we can take a stand against violence. We can begin by:

* Refusing to watch and refusing to let our children and grandchildren watch TV programs or movies that celebrate violence or pornographic sex, boycotting the products of programs' sponsors — and writing them letters telling them what we are doing and why.

* Forbidding toys in the house that represent violence, such as guns, rubber knives and swords, and similar objects.

* Quitting jobs whose main product is the destruction of human life, such as bombers, missiles, or handguns.

* Reading spiritual books that support our witness, such

as the slim works of Mother Teresa or Thomas à Kempis's fifteenth-century classic, *The Imitation of Christ.*

❈ Protecting our land by keeping it clean, recycling products, and teaching our children to do so.

❈ Speaking out in daily life to let others know that we work for a culture of love, not a culture of death.

Once I attended a formal dinner at which one of the leaders of a professional association was presented with a hunting rifle in appreciation for his services. Before I really knew what I was doing, I stood up, put my white linen napkin down on the table, and walked out of the room, my heels clicking on the floor. I stayed out until I was sure the award ceremony was over, then reentered the room.

Yes, the people at my table stared when I got up and when I came back. Yes, they asked me questions. Yes, I was nervous and my voice and stomach fluttered when I replied. "I don't believe in guns," I said. "I don't approve of this ceremony, and so I left."

It was so awkward. Someone else would have done it better, done it without a shaking voice. It really wasn't much of a witness, but it was mine. It wasn't easy for me to do; but then witness usually isn't.

Will's Smile

A glad heart makes a cheerful countenance. — Proverbs 15:13

The morning had not gone well. I'd learned the doctor was again having trouble controlling my dad's high blood pressure with medication, there was a mistake in my bank balance, and the white paint was peeling and flaking off again on the living room ceiling under the shower in the upstairs bathroom. I'd have to call or go to the bank, and try to find a painter who could, once and for all, get that ceiling to stop peeling.

Oh, well, I thought, putting aside my checkbook. *I'll work on this bank balance later.* As I stuffed my grocery list in my pocket and shut the front door, I saw Will, the little blond Down's syndrome boy in the yard across the street, waving at me from the arms of his caregiver and smiling broadly. Although Will was now three and a half, he looked to be about two. In addition to being retarded, he'd been in and out of hospitals since his birth for heart and lung problems, was deaf, and could not walk.

I knew that some of Will's operations had caused him severe pain, pain that could rightfully make him wary of adults. But I had never seen Will without a smile on his delicate little face with its pale skin and pointed chin. I had frequently seen him waving to neighbors, and I had watched as he stretched out his thin little arms toward grandparents and visiting friends.

I just don't have time for you today, Will, I thought as I headed for the car door. But something made me glance up before sliding into the driver's seat. Will was still waving, and his little mouth was fixed in that broad smile. I stopped and looked at Will, and as I did so, I felt my facial muscles relaxing. I was conscious that my own lips were turning up in a smile. I must have been frowning like an old sobersides, I thought, and still Will smiled at me. If this little handicapped child could give me a smile from his heart when I didn't deserve it, wasn't a hug the least I could give back to him?

I shut the car door, waved at Will, and headed across the street to ask his caregiver if I could hold him for a while. Will nestled against my shoulder and I felt the warmth of his body. He smelled faintly of milk and baby powder, and he was as light as a child just learning to walk. Will gurgled something close to my ear, and I replied, "Will, you're a wonderful boy, and I'm so glad to see you today." I meant it. I looked into his eyes and he looked into mine; now Will was smiling even more broadly. He didn't squirm and he didn't reach for my hair; he just stayed in my arms, content to be held. And I was content to hold him.

Lord, please help us always to make time in our lives for Your special, loving people, people who can coax us into smiling when we don't feel like it.

When Tradition Counts

At one time, the ads might have been tempting. As I leafed through the back of a New Age magazine recently out of curiosity, I thought about how I could have chosen any one of these New Age remedies for my soul sickness after Jim's death or after Rudy's death. At my most vulnerable, I would have done almost anything to end the pain. *Almost* anything.

After all, look what the ads promised: "an advanced metaphysical contact of interest to the serious seeker"; "a channeled entity whose perspective, techniques, and love have helped thousands move beyond limitations and into the celebration and joy of growing"; "healing with color and sound"; finding "the zodiacal relationship of the cosmos within each individual being"; "visual massage that is so real you can almost feel it"; and "awakening to your dream self." And I hadn't even gotten to the classifieds, which offered biodynamic agriculture; anthroposophic medicine; spiritual science (a contradiction?); magical healing herbs; a life energy charging device; subliminal health affirmations; crystal balls and pyramids; a "dream pillow" filled with mugwort (any of several wormwood herbs — I looked it up) and magical spices "to promote magical dreams every night"; speaking directly with the "Enlightened Sage Nome"; and analysis through numerology.

I had a choice: I could have sent Hank Harris on his way when the young assistant pastor came to me after Jim was killed. In my rage and despair, I could have said "no" and turned my back on God. I could have turned to any of these New Age remedies or joined a spiritual cult. But would any of them have worked?

The Old Testament is replete with stories of human beings both following and not following the dictates of their God. From earliest times, those who persist in a godly and righteous life are rewarded, like Noah and his family. Those who ignore God's laws are punished, like the multitudes who perished in the great flood. "Now the earth was corrupt in God's sight, and the earth was filled with violence. And God saw the earth, and behold, it was corrupt; for all flesh had corrupted their way upon the earth" (Genesis 6:11-12).

The Old Testament is also specific in what God expects

from us. In Leviticus 19, He very plainly sets out rules for righteous believers to follow: He forbids theft, lying, profanity, persecution of the handicapped, slander, hatred, cross-breeding of animals, adultery, the eating of blood, incest, tattoos, the consulting of mediums and wizards for advice, turning one's daughter into a prostitute, and all manner of heathen customs. God makes it clear that His chosen people are a holy people, and that those who believe in Him are different from others by the traditions, laws, and customs that shape their lives and worship.

Jesus, in chapters 5 through 7 of Matthew, clarifies how people who follow Him are to lead their lives. The Beatitudes (Matthew 5:3-11) very specifically describe the qualities of character Jesus expects of His followers. The Beatitudes are a prescription for happiness. The rules that follow the Beatitudes are a blueprint for living in harmony with oneself, one's neighbor, and all of the natural world. The New Testament makes it clear that as a people we human beings were taught by our Lord the consequences of sinful behavior and the catastrophes that can result when men and women heedlessly pursue self-focused ends.

The consequences of unbridled, selfish sexuality are disease, including AIDS, which is fatal; adultery, leading to the breakup of marriages and traumatized children; and unwanted, drug-addicted babies born out of wedlock who grow up in rootless non-family environments, including the street. Take a walk in any major city in the United States; human wreckage caused by alcoholism, drug abuse, lack of self-esteem, and parental neglect are all too evident on many street corners. Much of this wreckage was created when moral teaching and traditional rules of conduct were ignored.

Over the centuries, men and women came to appreciate that when they followed wise laws, customs, and traditions, they were happier, healthier, and felt closer to God. When these traditions were ignored, in contrast, they were done so at great peril. When we followed the devices and desires of our own hearts — without listening to the voice of God speaking to us through our consciences — too often we ended up in disaster. Since the time of Abraham, obedience to God has been a path to peace; rebellion and willfulness have led to destruction.

Today the Christian church stands as one of the last institutional bastions of tradition. Along with Judaism and the other traditional religions of the world, it remains a source of guidance and strength for a world badly battered by the transgressions of inhabitants who forget they were created in God's image. The church also remains a spiritual refuge and personal house of rebirth for people like me, people who turn to it in pain for the salvation of their souls.

But traditional religions have enemies, and vulnerable people like me must be warier than ever before of false prophets masquerading as truth sayers. New Age buzzwords about love, crystals, and therapy with scents and massage all have a certain popular appeal to people who are hurting or empty inside — especially if these commercial panaceas are readily accessible and please the senses. More destructive are cults and sects that play games with the mind, not the senses. It is no accident that cult deprogrammers have found their business picking up.

I believe that for seekers like me, all of these modern offerings in the guise of spirituality are no substitute for the word of God. Somehow I sensed that beneath the surface of some of the most appealing cults I would find fuzzy thinking; exclusivism; punitive rules that could lead to shunning; an "us against them" mind-set leading to paranoia; and even a destructive undercurrent that could lead to mass suicide. We are all part shadows and part light; I sensed that there was a deeper darkness in the shadows of some of the New Age offerings that could pull me down. Although I felt the seduction of that darkness when I was in pain, I chose to return to the roots of my Christian upbringing and align myself with the light.

No one ever said that trying to follow a traditional life of godliness was easy or a guarantee of happiness, least of all Jesus Himself. I could have told Him "no." But who would I be today? Human experience, in all its pain, beauty, waywardness, and searching, teaches us the wisdom and value of seeking our Creator on earth through the godly glimpses He has put in our path. It is our privilege to discern them and be attuned to the messages of hope they bring us.

Epilogue

I am making peace with the memories that sear and trying to be attuned to godly glimpses with heightened sensibilities. I spend more time now at church potlucks and in small study groups. There I can share, learn, comfort and be comforted, and draw closer to the Presence that guides my life.

Pungent scents of Chesapeake Bay marsh or a man's tool-stocked garage, and certain scenes of woods in snow or sailboats on choppy water, striped rugby shirts with white collars, a frolicking black-and-white border collie, or a tall man striding along in brown suede hiking boots still have the power to bring me up short. When they do, I am momentarily thrust back in time, and I forget where I am and who I am now.

Recently I had a dream that will, I believe, be repeated and drive the screaming, swooping predatory creatures of the Bald Mountain dream from my mind forever. This is the new dream:

A tall man with shadowed face is walking toward me, with light behind him. His hands are stretched out, palms up. I open my arms to him, wanting union with this shadow lover.

In the dream I speak to him: "So it was you. It was you all along." Now the shadow on his face lifts; the light seems to come from within his face, and it is so bright — bright as a sunspot — that in my dream I don't know why I'm not blinded. I can't look at his face, but I can't seem to look away. Why can't I see his features?

Is it Jim's face?

Is it Rudy's face?

And now I think I can almost see the eyes through this brightness that fills my dream, not deep-sea eyes like Jim's or brown winking-star eyes like Rudy's. These eyes pull me toward my shadow lover. They woo, they console, they seek. He wants me, I know he wants me to come to him. I walk faster, and this time in the dream I seem to be coming closer to his outstretched arms. And now I think I can almost see his face. It's not Jim's face, it's not Rudy's face, it's the luminous face of —

I wake from the dream. Outside, birdcalls warble of morning opportunities. Standing at the window of my bedroom I pull up the shade and push up the window's glassed lower half so I can hear what the cardinals and mockingbirds are calling out more clearly. Their trills — *whit-year, whit-year,* and *chiree, chiree, chiree* — fill the air. In my backyard, sunlight descends in one pure, strong shaft through the tree branches, touching the leaves selectively where it falls as the leaves shiver in the breeze, creating a pattern of shifting dark greens and lighter greens, a changing panorama of brightness and shadow. The delicate, regularly spaced veins and saw-toothed edges of the fluttering beech leaves are illuminated by the sunshaft's path.

The birdcalls of this new-breeze morning seem to float down the sunshaft straight to my window.

Scriptural Resources

Godly Glimpses
for Special Times

Turning to God's Word

When We Feel Abandoned by God

John 14:1-31; Job 37-42; Psalms 22, 80, 102, 116, 120, 121, 123, 130, 142.

John 14:1-31. This passage from John contains the words of Jesus that brought me solace after Jim died as I read it over and over: "I will not leave you comfortless: I will come to you" (v. 18, *King James Version*).

Job 37-42. The verses from Job address Job's anguished questioning of a fate he feels is unjust, and God's famous answer "out of the whirlwind" (38:1); God's response to Job says, in effect, take heart in knowing that I am the Lord of all, and that while you can question Me, you cannot know or understand My ways. Unlike the personal lines of comfort Jesus speaks in John, God's answer in the Job verses gives a far more global picture of mankind's place in God's universe: We are part of the whole pattern of creation, not the only creatures here, and our concerns are not the only concerns that count. The entire Book of Job, not just these verses, pertains to anyone who feels God no longer cares.

Psalms 22, 80, 102, 116:1-9, 120, 121, 123, 130, 142. The Psalms cited here are cries from the heart uttered by people who, like those in all ages of history, have known the despair of abandonment and turn to the Lord for help. Psalm 102 contains the age-old plea "Do not hide thy face from me in the day of my distress!" (v. 2).

Offering Thanksgiving

Luke 1:46-55 (the "Magnificat" of Mary); Song of Solomon 2:10-17; 1 Chronicles 29:10-13 (David's prayer of thanksgiving); Psalms 71, 89, 98, 103, 107, 148, 150.

Luke 1:46-55. In Mary's lovely "Magnificat," the young virgin, who has declared herself the Lord's "handmaiden" (v. 48), gives thanks to God for His goodness out of a truly gracious heart. She does not question Him or the mission He gives her, despite her knowledge that having a child out of wedlock was a sin that could cost her her coming marriage and her life.

Song of Solomon 2:10-17. This passage from Solomon

contains the lyrical lines that give thanks for the flowering of another spring: "For lo, the winter is past, / the rain is over and gone. / The flowers appear on the earth, / the time of singing has come . . ." (vv. 11-12).

1 Chronicles 29:10-13. David's prayer of thanksgiving is an effusive outpouring of gratitude. David gives thanks for God's power, glory, victory, and majesty, and he ends with the words "And now we thank thee, our God, and praise thy glorious name" (v. 13). The verses following this prayer of thanksgiving continue David's theme of gratitude, and contain the familiar line "For all things come from thee, and of thy own have we given thee" (v. 14).

Psalms 71, 89, 98, 103, 107, 148, 150. The Psalms of thanksgiving give expression to the voices of human creatures who clearly want their God to take notice of them and know their gratitude for His goodness: "I will sing of thy steadfast love, / O LORD, for ever; / with my mouth I will proclaim thy faithfulness to all generations" (89:1).

Seeking to Know God

Exodus 17:1-7; Psalms 42, 48, 50, 63, 77, 84, 95, 141; Isaiah 55:1-13; Matthew 13:1-9, 18-23; Matthew 22:34-40; Matthew 25:31-46; Luke 24:13-35; John 17; Romans 5:1-17; 1 Corinthians 6:11-20; 1 Corinthians 15:20-28; 1 Thessalonians 5:1-10.

Exodus 17:1-7. The Exodus passage, an antidote to spiritual dehydration, describes how, at God's direction, Moses struck a rock in the Sinai desert with a staff that had struck the river Nile, and enough water gushed forth from the rock to satisfy the thirsty and despairing Israelites and their livestock.

Psalms 95, 42. Psalm 95 celebrates this miracle of the "rock of our salvation" (v. 1), which can refer both to the water gushing forth from the rock at Moses' bidding and to God as a firm rock that will not be moved in times of trouble. Psalm 42 also uses the image of water, likening the thirst of mankind for God to that of a thirsty hart (male deer) panting for the water from flowing brooks. The other Psalms cited here also describe the desire of human seekers to know their Creator.

Isaiah 55:1-13. The verses from Isaiah also use the metaphor of water: "Ho, every one who thirsts, / come to the waters" (v. 1), and "For as the rain and the snow come down from heaven, / and return not thither but water the earth" (v. 10). These verses also contain God's answer to every seeker since Job: "For my thoughts are not your thoughts, / neither are your ways my ways, says the LORD. / For as the heavens are higher than the earth, / so are my ways higher than your ways / and my thoughts than your thoughts" (vv. 8-9). God is reminding us that although He wants us to seek Him as His loving children, there is a mystery at the very heart of the relationship between human beings and their Creator; we do ourselves and Him a disservice when we try to reduce Him to our level. If we could know Him fully, then we would be God.

Matthew 13:1-9, 18-23. In the parable of the sower, Jesus describes the fate of seeds cast upon the ground, pointing out that only the seeds that fall upon good soil bring forth grain. We are to be those fruitful seeds that bring forth the grain of good works — not the seeds on the path devoured by birds, or the shallowly rooted seeds that sprang up too early and were scorched and killed by the sun, or the seeds choked by thorny bushes.

Matthew 22:34-40. These verses give us God's first and second great commandments, "You shall love the Lord your God with all your heart, and with all your soul, and with all your mind. This is the great and first commandment. And a second is like it, You shall love your neighbor as yourself" (vv. 36-39). Seekers after God are to start here.

Matthew 25:31-46. Jesus reveals Himself here on the most basic human level, so that His followers can understand that when they feed the hungry, clothe the naked, and give shelter to the homeless, it is as if they are doing all these good works to the Lord Himself. To know God, Jesus is saying, is to serve others as if one were serving the Savior: "As you did it to one of the least of these my brethren, you did it to me" (v. 40).

Luke 24:13-35. These verses tell of the incident on the road to Emmaus, when two of Jesus' disciples did not know Him upon His appearance to them after the crucifixion. When their hearts are softened, their eyes are opened to His identity. Implicit in the story is our frequent blindness to the presence and message of Jesus in our daily lives.

John 17. This chapter is about oneness with God. Shortly before He is delivered to Pontius Pilate, Jesus asks God to keep

His followers safe, because "they are not of the world, even as I am not of the world" (v. 16). He describes the bond between Him and those who will be left behind to spread the good news of salvation: "The glory which thou gavest me I have given to them, that they may be one even as we are one" (v. 22).

Romans 5:1-17. These passages from Paul's letter to the Romans celebrate the message that mankind is justified by faith alone (vv. 1-2), not by any human deeds; we were given salvation as a free gift of grace, and cannot earn it. The verses also explain how Christ's death reconciled sinful humankind with God (vv. 9-17).

1 Corinthians 6:11-20. This passage describes the body as a holy temple for the Lord, which must not be defiled by sinful living: "Do you not know that your bodies are members of Christ? Shall I therefore take the members of Christ and make them members of a prostitute? Never!" (v. 15).

1 Corinthians 15:20-28. These verses give us the resurrection promise: "For as by a man came death, by a man has come also the resurrection of the dead. For as in Adam all die, so also in Christ all shall be made alive" (vv. 21-22).

1 Thessalonians 5:1-10. Here Paul tells the followers of Christ that they are children of the light and the day (goodness), not the dark and the night (sin), and he exhorts the Thessalonians to "put on the breastplate of faith and love, and [don] for a helmet the hope of salvation" (v. 8).

Psalms 42, 48, 50, 63, 77, 84, 95, 141. Reading these Psalms brings us closer to God through the words of people who sought him many years ago as we do today. They tell of "His holy mountain, beautiful in elevation" (48:2); an omnipotent God who claims His own creation: "For every beast of the forest is mine, / the cattle on a thousand hills. / I know all the birds of the air, / and all that moves in the field is mine" (50:10-11); a God who issues an irresistible call to His human children: "How lovely is thy dwelling place, / O LORD of hosts! / My soul longs, yea, faints / for the courts of the LORD; / my heart and flesh sing for joy / to the living God" (84:1-2).

For Times of Crisis

Psalms 18, 23, 25, 27, 31, 34, 42, 43, 46, 57, 61, 69, 70, 71, 102, 116, 131; Jeremiah 15:15-21; Jeremiah 20:7-13; Hosea 6:1-6; Matthew 10:16-33; Luke 22:41-45.

The Psalms I've cited here give us a spiritual anchor when our world seems to have collapsed, or when we face a dreaded task we don't think we can accomplish. The Twenty-third Psalm, perhaps the best known of all of these, gives us the comforting metaphor of Jesus as the good shepherd, leading His sheep beside still waters, giving them rest in green pastures and thus restoring battered souls. Psalm 102 is a protracted cry of distress from a human sufferer — beset on all sides by enemies — whose "bones cleave to my flesh" (v. 5) and who is like withering grass. In this Psalm the writer turns to the Lord for pity and mercy and as the only enduring help in the midst of change and chaos. The Psalm that started as a cry of agony ends on a hopeful note: "The children of thy servants shall dwell secure; / their posterity shall be established before thee"(v. 28).

Jeremiah 15:15-21. The prophet Jeremiah calls upon the Lord to remember him in his distress, reminding Him that he, Jeremiah, "ate" the words of the Lord like food, and they "became to me a joy / and the delight of my heart" (v. 16). With this word-food for meat, cries the prophet, "Why is my pain unceasing, / my wound incurable, / refusing to be healed? [And, he asks accusingly,] Wilt thou be to me like a deceitful brook, / like waters that fail?" (v. 18). This passage, like many of the Psalms of distress, ends on a saving note: "I will deliver you out of the hand of the wicked, / and redeem you from the grasp of the ruthless" (v. 21).

Jeremiah 20:7-13. In this passage the prophet begins by accusing the Lord of deceiving him: "I have become a laughingstock all the day; / everyone mocks me" (v. 7). But the passage ends with an affirmation of the hope of deliverance: "Sing to the Lord; / praise the Lord! / For he has delivered the life of the needy / from the hand of evildoers" (v. 13).

Hosea 6:1-6. Hosea prophesies how the Lord will rescue those who love Him: "After two days he will revive us; / on the third day he will raise us up, / that we may live before him" (v. 2).

Matthew 10:16-33. In these well-known Gospel verses, Matthew describes how the disciples are to be sent out to do the Lord's work — innocent, without arms or defenders, but protected because their attackers can never kill their souls.

The passage begins, "Behold, I send you out as sheep in the midst of wolves; so be wise as serpents and innocent as doves" (v. 16).

Luke 22:41-45. Drawing apart from the disciples on the Mount of Olives, Jesus, facing certain death on the cross, prays to have this burden lifted from Him if it can be done: "Father, if thou art willing, remove this cup from me; nevertheless not my will, but thine, be done" (v. 42). As He prays earnestly — sweat falling "like great drops of blood" on the ground (v. 44) — an angel of the Lord comes to Him, strengthening Him for the trial, pain, and suffering ahead.

Grieving a Loss

Ecclesiastes 3:1-8; Jeremiah 31:9-14; Isaiah 53:3-9; Matthew 5:1-12; Matthew 6:25-34; John 14; Romans 8:18-39; Revelation 7:13-17.

Ecclesiastes 3:1-8. The famous, rhythmical section from Ecclesiastes on the seasonality of the human experience — "For everything there is a season, and a time for every matter under heaven" (v. 1) — assures the griever that the time of weeping will not last a lifetime. For, according to this wise Old Testament preacher, there is surely "a time to weep, and a time to laugh; a time to mourn, and a time to dance" (v. 4). We are meant to mourn during the time of mourning, but not forever. We are meant to weep during the time for weeping, but not forever.

Jeremiah 31:9-14. Here the prophet — whose words of woe found their way into the English language as a "jeremiad" (extended lamentation) — offers hope to the mourner whose days are filled with tears: "With weeping they shall come, / and with consolations I will lead them back, / I will make them walk by brooks of water, / in a straight path in which they shall not stumble" (v. 9).

Isaiah 53:3-9. The image of the suffering servant — often cited as evidence that this Old Testament prophet foretold the coming of the Messiah — depicts the suffering servant who Himself knew grief for our sake, and who can comfort us because He has walked the sorrowing paths we walk. This is the "man of sorrows" passage: "He was despised and rejected by men; / a man of sorrows, and acquainted with grief; / and as one from whom men hide their faces / he was despised, and we esteemed him not. / Surely he has borne our griefs / and carried our sorrows" (vv. 3-4).

Matthew 5:1-12. This part of Jesus' Sermon on the Mount, known as the Beatitudes, distills His message of loving salvation into words that comfort the grieving heart: "Blessed are the poor in spirit, for theirs is the kingdom of heaven. / Blessed are those who mourn, for they shall be comforted" (vv. 3-4). The passage reminds us at the end that our reward for suffering is not of this earth, and that, like the prophets who went before us, we will join rejoicing throngs in heaven.

Matthew 6:25-34. These words of Jesus are balm for the anxieties and worries about the future that often plague someone grieving the loss of a loved one, especially a husband or wife. They tell us not to be anxious about the trappings of this life: "Look at the birds of the air: they neither sow nor reap nor gather into barns, and yet your heavenly Father feeds them. Are you not of more value than they? And which of you by being anxious can add one cubit to his span of life? . . . Consider the lilies of the field, how they grow; they neither toil nor spin; yet I tell you, even Solomon in all his glory was not arrayed like one of these" (vv. 26-29).

John 14. When Christ tells His disciples that He will never leave them and will prepare a place for them in heaven in His Father's house, He is speaking to us, too. The assurance that He is caring for our loved ones in heaven and will care for us when we join them in death can bring some measure of comfort to even the most desolate mourner. The passage couples beautiful poetic imagery with Jesus' passionate conviction of His Father's love.

Romans 8:18-39. Here Paul, onetime persecutor of Christians who has been converted into a passionate follower of Jesus' teachings, assures grievers that present sufferings are as nothing compared to the glory that is to come, and that nothing, not even death, "will be able to separate us from the love of God in Christ Jesus our Lord" (v. 39). Paul reminds us that God did not spare His own Son, but gave Him up so that we might be saved from ourselves through Him.

Revelation 7:13-17. This lyrical passage assures us that one day we will be in a glorious new world where suffering is no more: "For the Lamb in the midst of the throne will be their shepherd, / and he will guide them to springs of living water; / and God will wipe away every tear from their eyes" (v. 17).

When We Overflow with Joy and Praise
Psalms 65, 66, 71, 95, 98, 100, 104, 144, 145, 146, 147, 148, 149, 150.

The Psalmists knew how to express joy and praise their Lord in high-spirited words that leap off the page. They give us a forum to express ourselves when we're fairly bursting with exuberance, and invite us to raise our voices in praise. Psalm 95, known as the "Venite," is an extended expression of joy in creation: "O come, let us sing to the LORD; / let us make a joyful noise to the rock of our salvation!" (v. 1).

Psalm 100 is similarly passionate — "Make a joyful noise to the LORD, all the lands!" (v. 1) — while Psalm 149 invites those who have been through the dark night of the soul and come out into the light to "sing to the LORD a new song" (v. 1). Some years after my husband Jim's death, when I wanted to express gratitude to God for guiding me out of the pit of despair, I found a Christmas card with the words "Sing to the Lord a new song" on it. I sent it out in the mail to tell my friends that my heart was able to sing again.

Offering Blessings and Benedictions
Numbers 6:24-26; Psalm 19:14; 1 Corinthians 1:3; 2 Corinthians 13:14; Philippians 4:7-9; Revelation 1:4-6.

Numbers 6:24-26. This Old Testament blessing is as fitting today as it was centuries ago: "The LORD bless you and keep you: / The LORD make his face to shine upon you, and be gracious to you: / The LORD lift up his countenance upon you, and give you peace."

Psalm 19:14. In a Psalm of praise for the glory of God whose poetic imagery includes a tent set for the sun, "which comes forth like a bridegroom leaving his chamber" (v. 5), the writer ends with a peaceful benediction: "Let the words of my mouth and the meditation of my heart / be acceptable in thy sight, / O LORD, my rock and my redeemer" (v. 14).

1 Corinthians 1:3; 2 Corinthians 13:14. The passages from Paul's first and second letters to the Corinthians contain blessings that stress God's grace. It was Paul who reminded the early Christians in his letters that they — and we — are saved by grace alone, not by anything any human being can do on his or her own.

Philippians 4:7-9. In his letter to the Philippians, Paul — who refers to the Philippians as "my brethren, whom I love and long for" (v. 1) — blesses his readers as he wishes for them "the peace of God, which passes all understanding" (v. 7).

Revelation 1:4-6. John the divine, writing to the seven churches in Asia, greets them with a poetic passage that we may use today for blessings and benedictions: "Grace to you and peace from him who is and who was and who is to come, and from the seven spirits who are before his throne, and from Jesus Christ the faithful witness, the firstborn of the dead, and the ruler of kings on earth" (vv. 4-5). As the "first-born of the dead," Jesus — like the firstborn in a faithful, God-fearing family — is the best and the brightest hope for all His people. We mortal beings, His earthly people who have ears to hear His word and believe what it says, are destined also to rise from the dead through His saving grace.

Identifying Your Own Godly Glimpses: Questions for Spiritual Reflection

1. Think of a time in your life when things were very wrong and your world looked as black as a moonless and starless night. Who or what helped to move you out of that blackness and toward the light?

2. Has an unexpected event in your life changed the course you had charted for yourself? Do you like the new direction?

3. In your times alone, have you ever felt the nearness of a presence you could not quite describe? Was the presence comforting? Awe-inspiring? Frightening? Did you want the experience repeated?

4. Have you ever had a dream or dreams in which you were being attacked by terrifying forces, and then someone or something in the dream saved you?

5. If you have suffered a disappointment or tragedy in your life, has it caused you to become more introspective and contemplative, and less concerned with the kind of material success the world celebrates?

6. In your dealings with people you meet in daily life, have you ever met someone who provided you with an insight that made you stop and think, "Aha, so that's what it's all about"?

7. In your family relationships, especially frustrating ones, have you ever felt that you were being provided patience and understanding from a power beyond yourself?

8. Have you ever done something — such as taken a job or moved — and felt very strongly that you were meant to do exactly that?

9. Have there been times in your life when you were rushed or hurried, but you paused and went out of your way to do something kind for someone else? Were you glad you did? Did it matter that it made you late?

10. Do you ever feel a longing for something you can't quite pinpoint, something that draws you no matter how happy you are with your life as it is?

Author's Invitation: Please Share Your Godly Glimpses with Me

I know there are readers out there who have also experienced godly glimpses in their lives, and I hope this book, especially the reflection questions, has started you thinking about them. These are times in your daily life when you felt God seemed to be nudging, directing, consoling, or supporting you. Often our godly glimpses are not dramatic; they can be as soft as a whisper or as delicate as a snowflake.

I'd love to hear from you about your godly glimpses. You may write me at the following address: Peggy Eastman, Godly Glimpses, Book Editorial, Our Sunday Visitor, 200 Noll Plaza, Huntington, Indiana 46750.

Godly Glimpses: Book Discussion Guide

by Peggy Eastman
Book Editorial, Our Sunday Visitor
200 Noll Plaza
Huntington, IN 46750
Call toll-free 1-800-348-2440, Ext. 2460, for sales and service.
Year 2000 Edition, Copyright © 1999 by Peggy Eastman.
(This guide may be photocopied for use in small groups.)

Dear reader,

I wish I could sit down with you in your group so we could share our thoughts and feelings in person. Since I can't be there, I've written this substitute on paper at the request of my friends in small groups. I wouldn't dream of trying to intrude on the discussions in your group in any way; what goes on in a group is sacred, and I'm sure you've found that your members become a family. What this guide is intended to do is to answer some of the questions people have asked me about my book *Godly Glimpses* and, hopefully, deepen your own personal and group spiritual journey through discussion with others. I've started with some background information drawn from the questions people ask.

Q: Was it hard to write such a personal book?
A: Yes, the personal cost was very high, because I had to probe into some areas of my life that were very painful as well as write about the wonderful times. To write about my husband Jim's death in a plane crash and my husband Rudy's death from cancer brought back waves of grief. All this happened in only nine years. But what I wanted to do was to bring people hope, so I was usually able to get past the personal pain and keep writing. I wanted to take the personal pain and chaos of my life and offer them up in some form that would be a gift.

Q: How long did it take you to write *Godly Glimpses*?
A: It took ten years, off and on. A lot of that time was spent trying to get my life back on some kind of track of normalcy and find my center of gravity, so I couldn't concentrate

well enough to sit down and just work on the book for days and months at a time. At one point I did stop writing this book entirely. I felt it was too intensely personal and revealing; it left me too emotionally naked. But then a sense of urgency swept over me, a feeling almost of being taken by the scruff of the neck, shaken, and set on the path of completing *Godly Glimpses*, no ifs, ands, or buts. It was scary, exhilarating, and directive; I have never experienced anything like it before or since. I think I had this experience because there is so much pain in the world; all we have to do is pick up our daily newspapers and read the headlines. I took this sense of urgency as a sign to keep on writing; so I did.

Q: How do you feel about the book now that it's written?
A: I feel a profound sense of gratitude to God for letting me write it.

Q: Did you ever consider concentrating just on grief and healing?
A: Yes, I've written quite a few articles on coping with grief. But I didn't want to write a book on this topic, which had been suggested to me. I felt that a whole book on grief would be too narrow in scope and leave out so much of life that matters to all of us. Even when I was at my lowest points I was able to appreciate the colors of a sunset and the bravery of a crocus poking up through the spring earth.

Q: Your stories are about real people, places, and animals, but you seem to use some fictional techniques, such as lots of description. Why?
A: I was trained as a fiction writer, have written short stories, and am working on a novel. So it was natural for me to bring fictional techniques to my nonfiction. I was searching for a format to tell the stories in *Godly Glimpses* and I came up with what I think of as a hybrid style that seems to work best for me. But more than this, I wanted at all costs to avoid a "preachy" or "churchy" style, and so fictional techniques just kept creeping in. I don't think it's any accident that the stories in the Bible can be read as literature; those master storytellers — Jesus at the top of the list — knew exactly what they were doing.

Q: How can we be sure the godly glimpses in our lives that we think come from God really do?

A: That's a good question, and I've spent a lot of time thinking about it. We can never be sure in the sense of proving factual truth, as people do with a mathematical formula or scientific experiment. But the experiences that gave rise to the stories in this book brought love, and I believe the very essence of God is love. Even in the events that brought pain, God found a way to show love.

Topics for Group Discussion

Part 1: Godly Glimpses That Heal the Heart

1. In the first story, "I Will Not Leave You Comfortless," the plane crash throws everyone involved, most of all me, into chaos. Any semblance of control I thought I had was suddenly, brutally, snatched away. Can you think of times in your life when you thought you had things perfectly organized and without warning the bottom dropped out? How did you cope with these feelings of being out of control? Is the control we think we have as human beings totally illusory? If so, who really is in control? Why is it so hard for us to relinquish control over our lives?

Have people in your group read the Bible verses from chapters 37 to 42 of Job, which address Job's anguished questioning of a fate he feels is undeserved. If ever anyone felt out of control, it was Job. How do the members of your group feel about God's answer to Job? When God says that human beings cannot know or understand His ways, can we interpret that to mean that we have to suspend our need to control and trust in His greater wisdom?

2. In the story "What Honey Knew," why was my father's little white cat such a comfort? It has been said that animals bring us unconditional love. What is conditional love? Have you ever been in a relationship that had strings attached? Why do relationships with strings attached make us so uncomfortable? If we have to earn our way into another's heart, is this really love? Do you think God loves us no matter what?

3. In the story "The Unhaunting of Bald Mountain," why do you think the visual representation of the witches' Sab-

bath from Walt Disney's classic movie *Fantasia* — with its swooping predatory black birds — had such a powerful effect on me as a child? Why did this visual sequence from the movie return to haunt me after Jim died? To what extent do we allow the fears we have to dominate us? When Hank Harris suggested to me that I rescript my terrorizing Bald Mountain dream, he was offering love as an antidote to my fear. Do you agree with him that love is the best antidote to fear?

Part 2: Godly Glimpses of Bountiful Blessings

1. In the story "The Stick on the Beach," why do you think only one child — the little girl in the unzipped pink jacket — was deeply troubled by the sight of the dead jellyfish floating on the tide in a tangled mass? Do we naturally tend to relate to cute, cuddly animals like kittens and puppies and not to other creatures? Have someone read aloud the passages in Genesis 1:20-25. How can we help children develop a reverence for all of creation?

2. In the story "That Which Remains," Uncle Rem retains an essential inner core of personhood despite his illness. Think of someone you know who is ill in mind or body. Is it often difficult to know when you are reaching that person? What helps? How can we help the most infirm among us to keep their dignity and feel part of the human family?

3. "Coming Home" also tells of mentally handicapped people, but the twins Will and Jamie are living in the community, not in a nursing home like Uncle Rem. Do you think passage of the Americans with Disabilities Act has achieved the goal of helping to integrate handicapped people more fully into the fabric of society? What steps can we take that aren't in any law to help the disabled feel a greater sense of belonging?

Part 3: Godly Glimpses of Everyday Faith

1. "Brian's Family Book" tells of the impact of the loss of a baby sister on a young child. While no one can really be prepared for this kind of loss, what did Brian have that helped strengthen him? How can we help young children to under-

stand the concept of God and His Son on their own level?

2. The disease AIDS has brought people face to face with the death of young, creative men and women. In "Saying Good-bye to Ronald," why did he and I never use the word "good-bye"? What helps to comfort people who are suffering from life-threatening illnesses? What doesn't help? How can we know the difference?

3. "The Visitor from Before Time" tells of the horseshoe crab, ancient creature that sheds its shell for a new one when its current shell is outgrown. What spiritual lessons can the horseshoe crab teach us about growth? Does it hurt to shed? Do we continue to miss what we let go? What helps ease the pain?

Part 4: Godly Glimpses in Daily Service

1. The story "Please Don't Touch" tells of partitioned park benches. Why do you think these benches were designed and built this way? The park benches are partitioned by physical metal dividers; do you think we have a tendency to use mental partitions for those who are different from us or strangers to us? How can we begin to remove these mental partitions and start accepting humankind as one family?

2. "Saving Throwaway Children" tells of Covenant House staffers' work with the children no one wants. What pressures on families today might lead children to feel unwanted and leave home or be forced out? What can we do in our own neighborhoods to make troubled teens feel wanted and needed?

3. We've all heard statements that it's better to give than to receive. In "Who Is the Giver?" the nun known as "Dr. Sister" says she stays in tiny poverty-stricken Tutwiler, Mississippi, because she receives more from her patients than she gives them. What do her patients give her? Have you ever gone out of your way to help someone less fortunate and felt that what you got back was much more than you gave? Why?